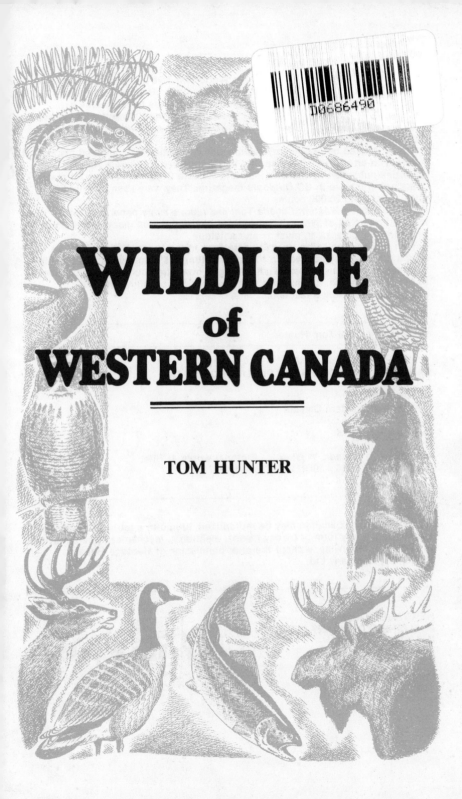

WILDLIFE
of
WESTERN CANADA

TOM HUNTER

THE AUTHOR

Tom Hunter was born in Powell River but spent his youth in Burnaby. He served in the Canadian Merchant Navy during World War Two and afterwards tried a variety of jobs but couldn't find one that suited him. Then in 1949 he enrolled in the Vancouver School of Art and on graduation 3 years later became a commercial artist. During his school years he supported himself with various summer jobs, one of them on the sternwheel steamer *Klondike*, last of the colorful paddlewheelers to ply the Yukon River.

The illustrated natural history feature was born when he combined his love of nature with artistic training. The first panel appeared in *Wildlife Review*, a magazine published by the B.C. Fish and Wildlife Department, then for many years was a feature in *BC Outdoors* magazine. They were then reprinted in a book which sold 25,000 copies.

For *Wildlife of Western Canada* Tom has redone every panel to provide information on all of Western Canada. He has also added many new species, including the polar bear, muskox and antelope.

Tom and his family live on a 6½-acre farm in the Fraser Valley about an hour's drive from Vancouver. In this rural setting his harmonious relationship with nature continues. Local wildlife ranges from birds such as Oregon juncos to the varied thrush, and animals from coyotes to opossum, with the occasional visit from a raccoon.

CANADIAN CATALOGUING IN PUBLICATION DATA

Hunter, Tom
  Wildlife of Western Canada

ISBN 0-919214-72-X

1. Zoology — Canada, Western — Pictorial works. I. Title.
QL221.W4H85 1986   591.9712   C86-091098-7

HERITAGE HOUSE
PUBLISHING COMPANY LTD.
Box 1228, Station A
Surrey, B.C. V3S 2B3

Printed in Canada

CONTENTS

OPOSSUM

THE OPOSSUM, ORIGINALLY NATIVE TO THE EASTERN UNITED STATES, WAS INTRODUCED INTO WASHINGTON IN THE 1920S AND BY THE LATE 1940S HAD MADE ITS WAY INTO B.C. NOW FIRMLY ESTABLISHED, ITS POPULATION INCREASES YEARLY.

ABOUT THE SIZE OF A HOUSE CAT, THE OPOSSUM LOOKS MUCH LIKE AN OVERGROWN RAT. WITH A THUMB-LIKE TOE ON EACH HIND FOOT AND A PREHENSILE TAIL, IT MOVES EASILY IN TREES TO SEARCH FOR FRUIT OR BIRDS' EGGS.

THE FEMALE HAS A POUCH INTO WHICH THE YOUNG CRAWL AT BIRTH WHEN THEY ARE NO LARGER THAN A HONEYBEE. THEY FASTEN THEMSELVES TO A TEAT AND REMAIN THERE UNTIL THEY ARE ABOUT THE SIZE OF MICE. THE FEMALE THEN TRANSPORTS THEM ON HER BACK WHILE TEACHING THEM HOW TO PROCURE THEIR FOOD.

WHEN THREATENED THE OPOSSUM MAY LIE DOWN AND PLAY DEAD, AND CAN REMAIN MOTIONLESS FOR HOURS.

FRONT FOOT

HIND FOOT

SHREWS

THERE ARE MANY SPECIES OF SHREWS IN WESTERN CANADA. THEY RANGE IN SIZE FROM THE LARGEST OF THE NORTH AMERICAN SHREWS, 15 CM (6 IN.) LONG, TO THE PYGMY SHREW, ONLY 8CM (3 IN.) LONG. THE PYGMY IS NORTH AMERICA'S SMALLEST MAMMAL, ITS WEIGHT ABOUT THAT OF A SODA CRACKER.

DESPITE ITS SIZE, THE SHREW IS THE MOST SAVAGE OF ALL MAMMALS AND EATS MORE THAN THREE TIMES ITS WEIGHT EVERY DAY. IN ITS RELENTLESS SEARCH FOR FOOD IT KILLS CREATURES TWICE ITS SIZE. ENERGY DERIVED FROM THE FOOD IS USED SO QUICKLY THAT IF A SHREW GOES WITHOUT FOOD FOR A DAY IT DIES. FOR THIS REASON IT EATS ANYTHING AVAILABLE.

THE NAVIGATOR SHREW, RIGHT, IS AN ACCOMPLISHED SWIMMER AND OFTEN FEEDS ON UNDERWATER LIFE.

HOUSECATS SOMETIME KILL BUT WILL NOT EAT A SHREW BECAUSE A MUSK GLAND ON THE SHREW'S STOMACH MAKES IT ALL BUT IMPOSSIBLE FOR THE CAT TO EAT.

PIKA

IN SPITE OF ITS SHORT, ROUND EARS AND INVISIBLE TAIL, THE PIKA IS A MEMBER OF THE RABBIT FAMILY. IT IS USUALLY FOUND HIGH IN THE MOUNTAINS WHERE IT LIVES IN OR NEAR A ROCK SLIDE. DURING THE SHORT ALPINE SUMMER THE PIKA GATHERS GRASS AND VARIOUS PLANTS AND SPREADS THEM A LAYER AT A TIME TO DRY. THIS "HAY" IS THE BASIS OF THE PIKA'S WINTER FOOD SUPPLY WHEN THE MOUNTAINS ARE COVERED IN MANY METERS OF SNOW. THE PIKA REMAINS ACTIVE THROUGHOUT THE WINTER AND, WEATHER PERMITTING, FEEDS ON LICHENS IN ADDITION TO ITS CACHE OF HAY.

THE PIKA IS CURIOUS BUT EXTREMELY SHY. IF AN INTRUDER GETS TOO CLOSE THE PIKA WILL LEAVE ITS ROCKY PERCH SO SWIFTLY THAT IT APPEARS TO VANISH. WHILE A FEW PIKAS FALL PREY TO HAWKS AND EAGLES, ITS CHIEF ENEMY IS THE WEASEL.

THE PIKA'S COLOR RANGES FROM ALMOST BLACK, TO LIGHT GREY, TO MANY SHADES OF BROWN. ITS COLORING MAKES IT ALMOST INVISIBLE AS IT SITS MOTIONLESS ON A ROCK.

JACKRABBIT

THE WHITE-TAILED JACKRABBIT, ONCE PLENTIFUL IN THE ARID LANDS BORDERING THE 49TH PARALLEL, HAS HAD ITS POPULATION GREATLY REDUCED BY FARMING AND OTHER ASPECTS OF CIVILIZATION.

THIS LARGE HARE WEIGHS FROM 3 TO 5 KG (6 TO 10 LBS.). IT IS GENERALLY PALE GREY WITH LIGHTER UNDERPARTS AND BLACK EAR TIPS. ITS LONG EARS AND LEGS DISTINGUISH IT FROM OTHER HARES AND RABBITS.

THE JACKRABBIT IS FOND OF GRAIN, ALFALFA AND GRASSES. AS A CONSEQUENCE, WHEN IT IS PRESENT IN LARGE NUMBERS, AGRICULTURAL DAMAGE MAY OCCUR. GENERALLY, HOWEVER, THE JACKRABBIT'S NATURAL ENEMIES, THE COYOTE AND THE LARGER HAWKS, KEEP IT IN CHECK.

SHARP EYES AND KEEN EARS ALERT THE JACKRABBIT TO IMPENDING DANGER AND ITS LONG SWIFT LEGS USUALLY ASSURE SURVIVAL.

SNOWSHOE HARE

SPECIES OF THE SNOWSHOE, OR VARYING, HARE ARE FOUND ALMOST EVERYWHERE IN CANADA. THE ANIMAL IS SO NAMED BECAUSE OF ITS LARGE HIND FEET WHICH COVER MORE THAN 30 SQUARE CM (12 SQUARE IN.) -- MINIATURE SNOWSHOES THAT MAKE TRAVELLING IN SNOW COMPARATIVELY EASY.

THE SNOWSHOE HARE HAS ALWAYS BEEN AN IMPORTANT SOURCE OF FOOD FOR MOST CARNIVOROUS MAMMALS AND LARGER BIRDS OF PREY. IN ADDITION, FOR CENTURIES THIS HARE HAS BEEN USED BY CANADIAN NATIVES TO AUGMENT FOOD SUPPLIES.

SPRING

SUMMER

IN SUMMER IT FEEDS ON VARIOUS PLANTS AND GRASSES BUT IN WINTER SWITCHES TO THE BARK OF YOUNG TREES. THE SNOWSHOE HARE, HOWEVER, NOT ONLY CHANGES ITS DIET WITH THE SEASONS BUT ALSO ITS COLOR. IN WINTER IT IS WHITE EXCEPT FOR EARTIPS AND EYELIDS; IN SUMMER, BROWN WITH WHITE UNDERPARTS.

MARMOT

THE HOARY MARMOT, OR WHIST-LER, SHOWN AT LEFT, INHABITS MOUNTAINOUS REGIONS OF B.C., ALBERTA, AND THE YUKON. ITS HOME IS USUALLY AN ALPINE AREA WHERE IT IS OFTEN SEEN LYING ON A ROCKSLIDE EN-JOYING THE SUN.

THE MARMOT IS ACTIVE FOR LESS THAN HALF THE YEAR, HIBERNATING THE REST OF THE TIME. IT FEEDS ON A VARIETY OF GRASSES AND PLANTS. MATING TAKES PLACE IN SPRING AND APPROXIMATELY THIRTY-FIVE DAYS LATER FOUR OR FIVE YOUNG ARE BORN.

THE WOODCHUCK, OR GROUNDHOG, SHOWN BELOW, IS ANOTHER SPECIES OF MARMOT BUT IT INHABITS GRASSLANDS AND AGRICULTURAL AREAS RATHER THAN MOUNTAINS. THE BURROW IS USUALLY AT THE BASE OF A TREE OR UNDER A ROCK, AND OFTEN EXTENDS WELL BENEATH THE SURFACE. THE GROUNDHOG IS NOT POPULAR WITH FARMERS IN SOME AREAS SINCE IT COMPETES WITH DOMESTIC ANIMALS FOR FORAGE.

ALL MARMOT SPECIES ARE STOUT BODIED AND HAVE SHORT BUSHY TAILS.

CHIPMUNK

CHIPMUNKS OF ONE SPECIES OR ANOTHER ARE FOUND ALMOST EVERYWHERE IN CANADA. THE SPECIES VARY ONLY A LITTLE IN APPEARANCE AND HABIT, AND TWO SPECIES CAN LIVE IN THE SAME LOCALITY WITHOUT INTER-BREEDING.

THE CHIPMUNK TAKES GREAT CARE IN THE CONSTRUCTION OF A BUR-ROW WHICH MAY SERVE AS BOTH STOREHOUSE FOR WINTER FOOD AND REFUGE AGAINST DANGERS OF THE OUTSIDE WORLD. THE BURROW IS USUALLY UNDER A LOG OR A BOUL-DER WHERE THE CHIPMUNK DIGS TO A DEPTH THAT WILL PROBABLY BE FROST FREE. IT THEN TUNNELS HORIZONTALLY, ADDING CHAMBERS FOR FOOD STORAGE AND A SLEEP-ING AREA. FINALLY, IT DIGS UP-WARD TO THE SUN TO PROVIDE A REAR EXIT. THE TUNNELS ARE LARGE ENOUGH TO ADMIT ONLY THE CHIPMUNK'S BODY, THUS GIVING IT PROTECTION FROM MOST ENEMIES.

THE CHIPMUNK IS LARGELY VEGE-TARIAN, FEEDING ON SEEDS, BERRIES, AND NUTS. ON OCCASION, HOWEVER, IT WILL ASCEND TO THE TREE TOPS IN SEARCH OF YOUNG BIRDS OR EGGS.

THREE TO FIVE YOUNG ARE BORN THIRTY DAYS AFTER MATING TAKES PLACE IN THE SPRING, THE YOUNG REMAINING IN THE BURROW FOR APPROXIMATELY ONE MONTH.

CHICKAREE

THE CHICKAREE, OR DOUGLAS SQUIRREL, INHABITS THE WEST SIDE OF THE CASCADE MOUNTAINS IN SOUTHERN B.C. IT USUALLY OCCUPIES AREAS ON THE EDGE OF CONIFEROUS FORESTS.

THE CHICKAREE IS OLIVE-BROWN WITH A BUFF UNDERSIDE. THESE TWO COLORS ARE SEPARATED BY A BLACK LINE ALONG ITS FLANK. THE CHICKAREE EATS SEEDS, BERRIES, FRUIT, MUSHROOMS, AND NUTS. IT ALSO ENJOYS CAMPSITE HANDOUTS. ALTHOUGH THE CHICKAREE IS AN AGILE TREE CLIMBER, IT SPENDS MUCH OF ITS TIME FORAGING ON THE GROUND.

THE CHICKAREE'S NEST IS USUALLY IN A HOLE IN A DEAD TREE AND IS LINED WITH MOSS AND STRIPS OF CEDAR BARK. SOMETIMES A WELL SHELTERED, ABANDONED BIRD'S NEST IS RENOVATED TO MEET ITS NEEDS. AN AVERAGE OF FOUR YOUNG ARE BORN IN EARLY SUMMER, WITH THE YOUNG ABLE TO FEND FOR THEMSELVES BEFORE WINTER.

FLYING SQUIRREL

THE FLYING SQUIRREL -- FOUND ACROSS CANADA EXCEPT FOR SOUTHERN SASKATCHEWAN AND MANITOBA -- INHABITS OPEN FOREST, BUT THOUGH IT IS PLENTIFUL, IS SELDOM SEEN. IT IS ACTIVE BETWEEN DUSK AND DAWN, AND NOT AT ALL DURING SEVERE COLD WHEN IT SLEEPS UNTIL THE WEATHER MODERATES.

THE FLYING SQUIRREL DOES NOT ACTUALLY FLY. IT GLIDES BY MEANS OF A MEMBRANE OF SKIN THAT EXTENDS FROM ITS FRONT TO BACK LEGS. LAUNCHING ITSELF FROM A TREE, IT CAN GLIDE MORE THAN 30M (100 FT.). AT THE END OF A GLIDE IT FLIPS UPRIGHT, LANDING WITH ALL FOUR FEET ON THE TRUNK OF ANOTHER TREE.

THE FLYING SQUIRREL'S NEST IS FOUND IN TREE BRANCHES OR IN A HOLE IN A TREE. TWO OR THREE YOUNG ARE BORN IN THE SPRING.

AS WITH OTHER SQUIRRELS, ITS DIET CONSISTS OF SEEDS, FRUIT, NUTS, LEAVES, AND, WHEN AVAILABLE, EGGS, YOUNG BIRDS, AND INSECTS. THE FLYING SQUIRREL, IN TURN, OFTEN FALLS PREY TO OWLS AND CATS BECAUSE OF ITS NOCTURNAL LIFE STYLE.

BEAVER

THE BEAVER IS FOUND ALMOST ANYWHERE THERE IS FRESH WATER. ITS WIDE, FLAT TAIL MAKES IT EASILY RECOGNIZABLE AND IS, OF COURSE, USED IN SWIMMING AND FOR SLAPPING THE WATER'S SURFACE TO WARN OF INTRUDERS.

THE BEAVER'S FOOD CONSISTS OF LEAVES, BARK, AND ROOTS OF VARIOUS TREES, AS WELL AS POND WEEDS AND DIFFERENT SHRUBS AND GRASSES.

MATING USUALLY TAKES PLACE IN MID-WINTER, WITH THE YOUNG BORN IN SPRING. THERE MAY BE FROM TWO TO EIGHT IN A LITTER. AT FOUR WEEKS THEY START ON SOLID FOOD AND AT SIX WEEKS ARE WEANED. BARRING ACCIDENT, DISEASE, OR MAN, A BEAVER MAY LIVE FIFTEEN YEARS OR MORE.

THE BEAVER'S LODGE IS CONSTRUCTED OF BRANCHES AND SMALL TREE TRUNKS PLASTERED WITH MUD. AN UNDERWATER ENTRANCE LEADS TO A SMALL DEN WITH AN AIR HOLE IN THE ROOF. CONSTANT REPAIRS TO THE LODGE AND DAM TAKE UP MUCH OF THE BEAVER'S TIME. A SMALL PILE OF BRANCHES IS USUALLY FOUND NEAR THE LODGE ENTRANCE FOR FOOD IN THE COLDER PART OF WINTER BECAUSE IT DOES NOT HIBERNATE.

THE BEAVER'S TEETH ARE ITS MOST IMPORTANT ASSET AND WITHOUT THEM IT WOULD BE UNABLE TO SURVIVE FOR VERY LONG. THE INCISOR TEETH NEVER STOP GROWING. CONSEQUENTLY, THE BEAVER MUST DO A GREAT DEAL OF CHEWING AND GNAWING TO KEEP ITS TEETH AT A WORKABLE LENGTH.

STOCKPILE OF BRANCHES

LODGE

AIR CHAMBER

DAM

ENTRANCE - EXIT

DEER MOUSE

THE NAME, DEER MOUSE, IS DERIVED FROM THE MOUSE'S BROWN AND WHITE COAT, LARGE EYES, AND BIG EARS. ALSO KNOWN AS THE WHITE-FOOTED MOUSE, IT IS FOUND ALL OVER CANADA, OFTEN IN AREAS OF HUMAN HABITATION. SEEDS, FRUIT, NUTS, GRASSES, INSECTS, AND A VARIETY OF OTHER FOODS ARE EATEN BY THIS SMALL RODENT. IN TURN IT IS PREYED UPON BY A GREAT VARIETY OF CARNIVORES.

SEVERAL LITTERS OF THREE TO SIX ARE BORN EACH SUMMER. THE NESTS ARE FOUND IN HOLLOW TREES, STUMPS, ABANDONED BIRDS' NESTS, OR ON THE GROUND.

SINCE THIS LITTLE MOUSE IS A CREATURE OF THE NIGHT, IT IS NOT EASILY OBSERVED. IN ADDITION, ITS COLORING AND SIZE MAKE IT EVEN MORE DIF-FICULT TO SEE.

IT IS A GOOD TREE CLIMB-ER AND OFTEN GOES ALOFT IN SEARCH OF BUDS, SEEDS, AND BERRIES.

MUSKRAT

THE MUSKRAT, A MEMBER OF THE RODENT FAMILY, IS USUALLY FOUND IN MARSHY AREAS ADJACENT TO RIVERS OR LAKES IN MOST PARTS OF CANADA. IN AND AROUND ITS WATERY DOMAIN IT FEEDS LARGELY ON PLANT LIFE BUT, ON OCCASION, WILL PARTAKE OF A FISH OR A FROG.

THE AVERAGE ADULT IS 50 CM (20 IN.) LONG AND WEIGHS ABOUT 25 KG (55 LBS.). THE MUSKRAT'S WARM DURABLE FUR HAS MADE IT CONTINUINGLY POPULAR FOR WOMEN'S FUR COATS.

THE MALE MUSKRAT PREFERS A SOLITARY LIFE, CONSORTING WITH THE FEMALE ONLY FOR SHORT BREEDING PERIODS. THE GESTATION PERIOD IS LESS THAN A MONTH, WITH SEVERAL LITTERS RAISED EACH YEAR. A LITTER RANGES FROM TWO TO TEN YOUNG, EACH LESS THAN 10 CM (4 IN.) LONG, BLIND, AND HAIRLESS. IN LESS THAN A MONTH, HOWEVER, THE YOUNG ARE WEANED AND EATING ON THEIR OWN.

THE MUSKRAT'S LEAF-LINED SLEEPING CAVITY IS AT THE END OF A BURROW IN A RIVER BANK OR IN A HAYCOCK IT HAS CONSTRUCTED. THE HAYCOCK IS MADE OF WEEDS, TWIGS AND MUD, AND SERVES AS WINTER QUARTERS AS WELL AS A NURSERY.

FRONT FOOT

HIND FOOT

PORCUPINE

ALTHOUGH THE PORCUPINE INHABITS MOST OF CANADA, IT IS RARELY SEEN ON THE PACIFIC COAST. IT IS PARTICULARLY FOND OF PINE FORESTS SINCE PINE BARK IS ITS FAVORITE FOOD. IT IS A GOOD CLIMBER AND HAS A BIG APPETITE, SO MUCH SO THAT IT SOMETIMES KILLS TREES WHEN IT EATS TOO MUCH OF THE BARK. IT ALSO DAMAGES AXE AND SHOVEL HANDLES BY EATING PORTIONS OF THEM. THE SALTY TASTE LEFT BY THE OWNER'S HANDS IS BELIEVED TO BE THE ATTRACTION.

THE TWO ILLUSTRATIONS ABOVE SHOW THE PORCUPINE IN A NORMAL, PASSIVE MOOD AND, AT RIGHT, IN A DEFENSIVE ATTITUDE. CONTRARY TO POPULAR BELIEF, IT IS NOT ABLE TO THROW QUILLS AT ITS ENEMIES. IT CAN, HOWEVER, STRIKE WITH ITS TAIL, LOOSENING QUILLS WHICH MAY BECOME ATTACHED TO ITS ADVERSARY.

THE QUILLS, THROUGH THE MUSCLE ACTION OF THEIR VICTIM, CAN WORK THEIR WAY 5 CM (2 IN.) INTO THE FLESH. THE AVERAGE PORCUPINE HAS SOME 30,000 QUILLS.

THE PORCUPINE'S DEN IS USUALLY IN A SMALL ROCKY CAVE OR HOLLOW STUMP. IT MATES IN EARLY WINTER AND AFTER A GESTATION PERIOD OF 112 DAYS A SINGLE BIRTH OCCURS. THE YOUNG PORCUPINE WEIGHS ABOUT 600 G (20 OZ.) AND IS APPROXIMATELY 25 CM (10 IN.) LONG. IN ONLY TWO DAYS IT IS ABLE TO CLIMB TREES AND IS USUALLY WEANED AFTER TEN DAYS. IT CAN GROW TO 1 M (3 FT.) AND WEIGH 8 KG (18 LBS.).

OTHER THAN MAN, THE ONLY ANIMAL INTERESTED ENOUGH TO PREY ON THE PORCUPINE IS THE FISHER.

SPERM WHALE

THE SPERM WHALE IS THE LARGEST OF THE TOOTHED WHALES. WHILE BULLS MAY REACH 20M (65 FT.), 12 M (40 FT.) IS ABOUT AVERAGE. THE COW IS USUALLY ONE-THIRD SMALLER.

A RESERVOIR OF OILY WAX IN THIS WHALE'S LARGE SQUARE NOSE IS BELIEVED TO BE THE REASON THAT IT CAN DIVE TO GREAT DEPTHS AND SURFACE QUICKLY WITHOUT GETTING THE BENDS.

AT TWO OR THREE YEARS OF AGE THE SPERM IS READY TO BREED. THE GES- TATION PERIOD IS APPROXIMATELY SIXTEEN MONTHS AND THE CALF IS CLOSE TO 4.5M (15 FT.) LONG AT BIRTH.

THIS WHALE'S DIET CONSISTS OF RAGFISH, SKATE, DOGFISH, AND ROCKFISH, BELOW, AND, ABOVE, GIANT SQUID.

KILLER WHALE

KILLER WHALES, SEEN HERE AT-
TACKING A GREY WHALE, ARE FOUND
ALL ALONG THE B.C. COAST AND
FREQUENTLY INVADE BAYS AND INLETS.
THEY TRAVEL IN SCHOOLS RANGING
FROM TWO OR THREE TO MORE THAN
ONE HUNDRED. IN COLOR THEY ARE
GENERALLY BLACK WITH WHITE AT
THE THROAT AND BELLY AND A
WHITE PATCH BEHIND
EACH EYE.

THEY HUNT WOLF-PACK STYLE,
ENABLING THEM TO KILL OR SEV-
ERELY INJURE MUCH LARGER WHALES.
HOWEVER, THEY MORE GENERALLY
PREY ON DOLPHINS, PORPOISES, SEALS,
SQUID, MANY KINDS OF FISH, AND
THE OCCASIONAL SEABIRD. THE
KILLERS' SWIMMING ABILITY, COU-
PLED WITH TEN TO THIRTEEN PAIRS OF
STURDY, CONE-SHAPED TEETH, MAKE
THEM HIGHLY EFFICIENT FOOD-GATH-
ERING MACHINES.

FEMALE

MALE

MATING TAKES PLACE ONCE A YEAR AND THE YOUNG, ABOUT 2M
(6 FT.) LONG, ARE BORN AFTER A GESTATION PERIOD OF TWELVE MONTHS. MALES
GROW TO 7.5 M (25 FT.) OR MORE WITH A DORSAL FIN AS HIGH AS 2M(6FT.).
FEMALES ARE SMALLER, USUALLY LESS THAN 6M (20 FT.), WITH A DORSAL FIN
ABOUT .6M (2 FT.) HIGH.

FINBACK WHALE

PERHAPS THE MOST GRACEFUL OF THE LARGE WHALES, THE FINBACK GROWS TO 25 M (8 FT.). IN APPEARANCE IT RESEMBLES THE GREAT BLUE WHALE, ALTHOUGH SMALLER AND SLIMMER. DURING THE SUMMER THIS LARGE WHALE FEEDS ON KRILL AND OTHER EUPHAUSIDS OFF THE B.C. COAST.

AT ONE TIME THE FINBACK'S SPEED AND AGILITY IN THE WATER OFTEN SAVED IT FROM THE WHALER'S HARPOON. HOWEVER, MODERN METHODS OF WHALING HAVE PROVED DEADLY AND FEW FINBACKS NOW FROLIC IN PACIFIC COAST WATERS.

BREEDING TAKES PLACE IN NORTHERN CLIMES DURING WINTER, WITH THE GESTATION PERIOD THOUGHT TO BE A LITTLE OVER ELEVEN MONTHS. THE BIRTH IS USUALLY SINGLE AND THE CALF 6 M (20 FT.) LONG.

BLUE WHALE

THE BLUE WHALE, THE LARGEST MAMMAL EVER TO INHABIT THE EARTH, IS SOMETIMES SEEN IN SMALL NUMBERS OFF THE B.C. COAST. THIS GIANT OF THE SEA IS A MEMBER OF THE RORQUAL FAMILY AND EASILY RECOGNIZED BY ITS LONGITUDINAL THROAT GROOVES. THE PURPOSE OF THESE GROOVES IS TO EXPAND, ACCORDION-STYLE, PERMITTING THE WHALE TO TAKE HUGE QUANTITIES OF FOOD, PLANKTON, IN ONE MOUTHFUL. THE PLANKTON IS CAUGHT IN THE CURTAINS OF WHALE-BONE, OR BALEEN, WHILE THE SEA WATER IS EXPELLED.

THE BLUE WHALE CAN TRAVEL AT 24 KPH (15 MPH) AND ONCE RANGED OVER ALL THE OCEANS OF THE WORLD IN GREAT NUMBERS. WHALING FACTORY SHIPS TOOK THOUSANDS OF BLUE WHALES EVERY YEAR AND BY 1960 ONLY AN ESTIMATED 2,000 SURVIVED. HOPEFULLY, TODAY'S CONSERVATION EFFORTS WILL SAVE THIS MAGNIFICENT MAMMAL FROM EXTINCTION.

BRACHIOSAURUS
45 TONNES (50 TONS)

GREAT BLUE WHALE
109 TONNES (120 TONS)

AFRICAN ELEPHANT
4.5 TONNES (5 TONS)

THE AFRICAN ELEPHANT AND THE LARGEST DINOSAUR WOULD BE DWARFED BY THIS WHALE.

COYOTE

IN WESTERN CANADA, THE COYOTE INHABITS MEADOW LANDS, PRAIRIES, AND OPEN FORESTS. ITS MOURNFUL HOWL IS PARTICULARLY FAMILIAR TO PEOPLE IN RURAL AREAS. IT IS USUALLY GREY AND LOOKS NOT UNLIKE AN UNDERFED GERMAN SHEPHERD DOG. IT WEIGHS UP TO 19 KG (42 LBS.), WITH THE MALES CONSIDERABLY LARGER THAN THE FEMALES.

COYOTE PUPS ARE BORN IN BURROWS, USUALLY FIVE OR SIX TO A LITTER, AFTER A GESTATION PERIOD OF ABOUT SIXTY DAYS.

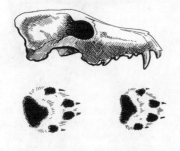

THE COYOTE LIVES MAINLY ON MICE, RABBITS, AND BIRDS, BUT ON OCCASION WILL EAT INSECTS AND EVEN FRUIT. YOUNG DEER AND SHEEP ARE ALSO TAKEN WHEN AVAILABLE. CONTRARY TO GENERAL BELIEF, THE COYOTE KILLS VERY LITTLE DOMESTIC STOCK. IT IS A CAPABLE RODENT HUNTER, HENCE OF VALUE TO FARMERS AND RANCHERS. IT IS ALSO ONE OF THE FEW ANIMALS FAST ENOUGH TO CATCH A RABBIT. COYOTES OFTEN HUNT IN PAIRS, ELIMINATING MUCH TRAVELING WHEN FOLLOWING THE ZIG-ZAG COURSE OF A RABBIT.

THERE ARE NO INCIDENTS ON RECORD OF AN UNPROVOKED COYOTE ATTACK ON MAN, ALTHOUGH THE REVERSE CAN- NOT BE SAID. NEXT TO MAN, THE COYOTE'S MAIN ENEMY IS ITS COUSIN, THE WOLF. THE COYOTE, LIKE THE WOLF, IS MUCH MALIGNED. IN REALITY IT IS NOT NEARLY SO VILLAINOUS AS CLAIMED.

WOLF

THE MUCH MALIGNED WOLF IS IN REALITY ANOTHER WILD CREATURE EARNING ITS KEEP THE HARD WAY. SINCE IT LIVES LARGELY ON DEER, MOOSE, CARIBOU, AND MOUNTAIN SHEEP, IT IS MOST POPULOUS WHERE THESE ANIMALS RANGE. THE LARGEST MEMBER OF THE DOG FAMILY IN THE WILD, IT INHABITS MOST OF THE WOODED AREAS OF WESTERN CANADA.

A WOLF USUALLY MATES FOR LIFE. BREEDING TAKES PLACE IN THE EARLY PART OF THE YEAR WITH THREE TO TWELVE PUPS BORN IN MAY OR JUNE. THE PUPS ARE RAISED IN AN UNDERGROUND DEN WITH BOTH PARENTS PARTICIPATING IN THE FEEDING AND TRAINING. THE PUPS AT ONE YEAR ARE AS LARGE AS THEIR PARENTS.

A MATURE WOLF CAN BE MORE THAN 2M (7 FT.) LONG AND WEIGH OVER 45 KG (100 LBS). THE WOLF IS A CHAMPION WHEN IT COMES TO ENDURANCE RUNNING. IN SEARCH OF FOOD, IT CAN LOPE ALL NIGHT AT 10 KPH (6 MPH), WITH A TOP SPEED CLOSE TO 18 KPH (30 MPH) AND TRAVEL 60 KM (100 MILES). THE WOLF IS ALSO AN EXCELLENT SWIMMER.

WOLF TRACKS ARE NOT UNLIKE THOSE OF A LARGE DOG.

THE WOLF'S MASSIVE SKULL IS EQUIPPED WITH POWERFUL JAWS AND A MOUTHFUL OF TEETH THAT SPECIALIZE IN RIPPING, TEARING, AND CRUSHING.

RED FOX

ONE SPECIES OR ANOTHER OF THE RED FOX IS FOUND ALMOST ANY-WHERE IN CANADA. THE FOX IN-HABITS THE FOREST EDGE IN PROX-IMITY TO FIELDS OR NATURAL CLEARINGS, ALTHOUGH ITS RANGE IS ONLY A FEW SQUARE KILO-METERS.

ODDLY ENOUGH, THE RED FOX IS OFTEN NOT RED AT ALL. IT MAY BE BLACK, SILVER, OR CROSS-- A COMBINATION OF BLACK AND RED THAT FORMS A CROSS DOWN THE RIDGE OF ITS BACK AND OVER ITS SHOULDERS. WHILE ALL FOUR COLOR PHASES CAN OCCUR IN ONE LITTER, BLACK APPEARS TO BE THE RAREST.

AS A VERMIN EXTERMINATOR THE FOX IS SUPREME, ALTHOUGH THIS SMALL MEMBER OF THE DOG FAMILY SELDOM WEIGHS OVER 6 KG (10 LBS.). ITS FOOD IS MAINLY RABBITS, MICE, AND RATS, BUT BIRDS, SNAKES, AND FROGS ARE ALSO RELISHED. UNFORTUNATELY, IT IS NOT AVERSE TO RAIDING CHICKEN PENS IF GIVEN THE OPPORTUNITY.

WHEN THE BREEDING SEASON IS OVER THE DOG FOX STAYS WITH HIS VIXEN UNTIL THE PUPS ARE OLD ENOUGH TO LEAVE HOME. THERE IS ONE LITTER PER YEAR, AVERAGING FOUR TO SIX PUPS. WHEN THE PUPS ARE ABOUT TWO MONTHS OLD THE MOTHER LEAVES THE DEN FROM TIME TO TIME TO ASSIST HER MATE IN FINDING FOOD.

BLACK BEAR

WHEN THE BLACK BEAR IS ENCOUNTERED IN THE WOODS OR AROUND A CAMPSITE IT SHOULD BE TOTALLY AVOIDED. IN SPITE OF ITS FRIENDLY AND CURIOUS APPEARANCE, IT CAN AT TIMES BE EXTREMELY DANGEROUS.

AN ADULT BLACK BEAR WEIGHS FROM 90 KG (200 LBS.) TO 270 KG (600 LBS.). BLACK BEARS ARE NOT ALWAYS BLACK. THEY ARE FOUND IN MANY SHADES OF BROWN AND, IN B.C., THERE IS EVEN A WHITE COLOR PHASE. ALL "BLACK" BEARS, HOWEVER, HAVE ONE THING IN COMMON -- IN ONE COLOR PHASE OR ANOTHER THEY INHABIT VIRTUALLY ALL OF CANADA.

WHILE THE GRIZZLY IS UNABLE TO CLIMB TREES BECAUSE OF ITS GREAT WEIGHT, THE BLACKIE SCOOTS UP THEM WITH EASE. IT IS AN OMNIVOROUS ANIMAL WITH LARGE, HEAVILY CONSTRUCTED CANINE TEETH IDEALLY SUITED TO A DIET OF MEAT, GRASSES, FRUIT, BERRIES, FISH AND INSECTS. THE PRIMITIVE STRUCTURE OF THE BEAR'S FEET EXPLAIN ITS PECULIAR SHUFFLING GAIT.

GRIZZLY

BRITISH COLUMBIA, ALBERTA, THE YUKON, THE NORTHWEST TERRITORIES, AND ALASKA CONTAIN PRACTICALLY ALL OF NORTH AMERICA'S GRIZZLY POPULATION. SOUTH OF THE CANADIAN BORDER A FEW HUNDRED REMAIN IN NATIONAL PARKS SITUATED IN THE NORTHWESTERN STATES.

THE GRIZZLY CAN BE EXTREMELY DANGEROUS TO MAN IF IT IS SUDDENLY DISTURBED AT CLOSE RANGE, OTHERWISE IT WILL SELDOM ATTACK. WHILE THE GIANT BEAR WILL OCCASIONALLY TAKE SICK OR CRIPPLED SHEEP, ELK, DEER, AND OTHER LARGE ANIMALS, ITS USUAL FARE IS MARMOTS, GROUND-SQUIRRELS, GRASSES, AND BERRIES.

THE LARGER OF THE TWO SKULLS SHOWN ABOVE BELONGS TO THE GRIZZLY. AS EVIDENT, IT IS SOMEWHAT LARGER THAN THAT OF ITS COUSIN, THE BLACK BEAR. THE GRIZZLY'S HIND FEET LEAVE TRACKS ABOUT 28 CM (11 IN.) LONG; THE FRONT FEET, USUALLY ABOUT 14 CM (5½ IN.) LONG.

AT BIRTH THIS MASSIVE BEAST WEIGHS ONLY .6 KG (1½ LBS.) AND IS ONLY 20 CM (8 IN.) LONG. AT MATURITY IT MAY WEIGH 270 KG (600 LBS.) OR MORE. THE CUBS STAY WITH THEIR MOTHER THROUGH THE FIRST SUMMER AND OFTEN LONGER.

YOUNG GRIZZLIES WILL CLIMB TREES TO ESCAPE DANGER OR JUST FOR FUN, BUT WHEN MATURE THEIR WEIGHT PROHIBITS SUCH ACTIVITY.

POLAR BEAR

THE POLAR BEAR INHABITS CANADA'S BARREN AND FRIGID NORTHERN FRINGE FROM THE YUKON TO LABRADOR. ITS ONLY ENEMY, APART FROM DISEASE OR INJURY, IS MAN WITH HIS HIGH-POWERED RIFLE.

A LARGE MALE POLAR BEAR IS ABOUT 2.75 M (9 FT.) LONG AND WEIGHS CLOSE TO 410 KG (900 LBS.), WITH SOME EXCEPTIONAL INDIVIDUALS WEIGHING UPWARDS OF 680 KG (1,500 LBS.).

IN SUMMER THE LARGE WHITE BEAR FEEDS ON WATERFOWL EGGS, BERRIES, GRASS, AND SEAWEED; WHILE IN WINTER IT TURNS TO THE SEA FOR SEALS, CRUSTACEANS, AND FISH. THESE FOOD SOURCES ARE SOMETIMES FORGOTTEN BY POLAR BEARS LIVING NEAR A NORTHERN SETTLEMENT, SUCH AS CHURCHILL, MANITOBA, WITH A GARBAGE DUMP.

IN EARLY FALL THE FEMALE POLAR BEAR HEADS INLAND TO DIG A DEN UNDER A SNOWDRIFT. HERE SHE CURLS UP FOR APPROXIMATELY FOUR MONTHS, WITHOUT FOOD OR WATER, BUT ABLE TO SURVIVE ON THE THICK LAYERS OF FAT BENEATH HER SKIN. THE CUBS, USUALLY TWINS, ARE BORN IN FEBRUARY. THEY ARE HAIRLESS, TOOTHLESS, AND BLIND, AND FOR SIX WEEKS DEPEND ON THEIR MOTHER FOR WARMTH AND NOURISHMENT. IN EARLY APRIL SHE BREAKS OUT OF THE DEN TO LEAD THEM DOWN TO THE SEA.

HIND FOOT

FRONT FOOT

RACCOON

THE MISCHIEVOUS AND CURIOUS RACCOON IS FOUND THROUGHOUT SOUTHERN CANADA, EXCEPT IN THE ROCKY MOUNTAINS. WITH ITS BLACK MASK AND RINGED TAIL, THE RACCOON CANNOT BE MISTAKEN FOR ANY OTHER ANIMAL.

ITS DIET CONSISTS OF A WIDE VARIETY OF FOODS WHICH INCLUDE FRUIT, RODENTS, FROGS, INSECTS, AND, WHEN NEAR WATER, FISH, CRABS, AND CRAYFISH. AN UNUSUAL CHARACTER TRAIT IS THAT IT WASHES ITS FOOD WHEN OPPORTUNITY PERMITS.

THE RACCOON IS AN EXCELLENT TREE CLIMBER AND SPENDS MUCH OF ITS TIME ALOFT SEARCHING FOR FRUIT AND BIRDS' EGGS. WHILE IT IS AN APPEALING LITTLE CREATURE, IT IS AT TIMES A PROBLEM FOR CHICKEN RANCHERS AND FRUIT FARMERS.

LITTERS AVERAGING THREE OR FOUR ARE BORN IN THE SPRING. THE MOTHER TRANSPORTS EACH OF HER YOUNG FROM ONE PLACE TO ANOTHER BY THE NAPE OF THE NECK, MUCH AS A CAT CARRIES A KITTEN.

MINK

THE MINK INHABITS ANY AREA CLOSE TO RIVERS, LAKES, STREAMS, OR THE OCEAN. AN EXCELLENT SWIMMER, IT EASILY AUGMENTS ITS DIET WITH A VARIETY OF MARINE LIFE.

BREEDING TAKES PLACE IN EARLY SPRING AND, AFTER A GESTATION PERIOD OF SIX WEEKS, UP TO TEN YOUNG ARE BORN. THE YOUNG ARE WEANED AT FIVE WEEKS AND LEAVE THE DEN AT SIX TO EIGHT WEEKS. AT THIS TIME THE MOTHER BEGINS TO TEACH HER OFFSPRING THE SKILLS OF KILLING, A LESSON THEY LEARN WELL.

MINK SKULL

FORE FEET

HIND FEET

MINK TRACKS

INCLUDING ITS TAIL, A FULLY GROWN MINK MAY MEASURE 72 CM (28 IN.) AND WEIGH 4 KG (2 LBS.). THE FEMALE USUALLY WEIGHS A LITTLE MORE THAN HALF AS MUCH AS THE MALE.

WOLVERINE

THE WOLVERINE, LIKE THE WOLF, IS MUCH MALIGNED WHEN STORIES ARE TOLD. BUT IS IT NOT JUST ANOTHER WILDERNESS CREATURE TRYING TO STAY ALIVE THE ONLY WAY IT KNOWS HOW?

THOUGH IT SELDOM WEIGHS MORE THAN 13 KG (30 LBS.), IT HAS BEEN CREDITED WITH BEING ABLE TO KILL A FULL-GROWN MOOSE OR ELK. SUCH TALES ARE MORE FOLKLORE THAN FACT, UNLESS THE MOOSE OR ELK IS SICK, INJURED, OR FOUNDERING IN DEEP SNOW. THIS LITTLE ANIMAL HAS AMAZING STRENGTH AND HAS BEEN KNOWN TO DRAG A CARCASS WEIGHING MUCH MORE THAN ITSELF OVER ROUGH, SNOW-COVERED COUNTRY FOR SEVERAL KILOMETERS.

THE WOLVERINE'S USUAL FARE CONSISTS OF SMALLER BIRDS AND MAMMALS SUCH AS GROUSE AND SQUIRRELS. WHEN NOTHING ELSE IS AVAILABLE IT WILL EAT SLUGS, SNAKES, AND FROGS. IT WILL STAY BY A CARCASS UNTIL EVERYTHING EDIBLE HAS BEEN DEVOURED. BECAUSE OF ITS POWERFUL DIGESTIVE SYSTEM WHICH IS ABLE TO DISPOSE OF FOOD FREQUENTLY AND EFFICIENTLY, IT HAS A MAMMOTH APPETITE. ITS LATIN NAME, "GULO," MEANS GULLET AND SUITS IT VERY WELL.

THE WOLVERINE IS FOUND IN THE MOUNTAINOUS AREAS OF B.C., ALBERTA, THE YUKON, AND THE NORTHWEST TERRITORIES. IT MATES IN EARLY SPRING AND SIXTY DAYS LATER TWO TO FOUR YOUNG ARE BORN. THE YOUNG STAY WITH THEIR MOTHER UNTIL FALL WHEN THE FAMILY DISPERSES.

WOLVERINE SKULL

THE POWERFUL JAWS AND RAZOR-SHARP CLAWS OF THE WOLVERINE, COUPLED WITH ITS GENERAL FEROCITY, MAKE IT A FORMIDABLE ADVERSARY.

BADGER

THE BADGER IS FOUND IN WESTERN CANADA'S PRAIRIE LANDS AND OPEN FOREST, USUALLY IN THE VICINITY OF GROUND-SQUIRREL POPULATIONS WHICH FORM THE MAIN PART OF ITS DIET. WHILE ITS POWERFUL FRONT CLAWS ASSIST IN DIGGING PREY FROM UNDERGROUND BURROWS, IT ALSO FEEDS ON BIRDS AND THEIR EGGS, MICE, AND SNAKES. THE BADGER STAYS CLOSE TO ITS BURROW DURING THE DAY AND DOES MOST OF ITS HUNTING AT NIGHT.

THE BADGER'S UNDERGROUND NEST IS FOUND AT THE END OF A TUNNEL THAT MAY EXCEED 10 M (33 FT.). AS MANY AS FIVE YOUNG ARE BORN IN LATE SPRING.

BADGER SKULL

WHILE THE BADGER IS UNABLE TO CLIMB TREES, SWIM, OR RUN VERY FAST, IT CAN DIG ITSELF INTO THE GROUND AND OUT OF SIGHT IN A FEW MINUTES. ADDITIONAL PROTECTION IS PROVIDED BY RAZOR-SHARP CLAWS AND TEETH, ENABLING IT TO EASILY FEND OFF DOGS, COYOTES, AND OTHER OF ITS NATURAL ENEMIES.

SPOTTED SKUNK

THE SPOTTED SKUNK IS MUCH SMALLER THAN ITS RELATIVE, THE STRIPED SKUNK. WHILE IT USES THE SAME METHOD OF SELF-DEFENCE, IT PREFERS TO EJECT ITS PUNGENT SPRAY WHILE DOING A HAND-STAND, OR "PAWSTAND." THIS LITTLE SKUNK HAS FEW ENEMIES. ONLY EAGLES OR LARGER OWLS DARE ATTACK IT.

IN THE SPRING THE FEMALE GIVES BIRTH TO THREE OR FOUR NAKED YOUNG AND WITHIN THREE WEEKS THEY GROW A THICK BLACK AND WHITE COAT.

THE SPOTTED SKUNK STAYS IN ITS BURROW IN THE DAYTIME, EMERGING AT NIGHT FOR FOOD. MICE, BIRDS, FROGS, SNAKES, FRUIT, AND INSECTS ARE ITS DIET, WITH INSECTS PRE-DOMINATING.

BECAUSE ABUNDANT UNDER-GROWTH IS THIS SKUNK'S PRE-FERRED HABITAT, IT IS SELDOM SEEN EAST OF THE PACIFIC COAST MOUNTAINS.

STRIPED SKUNK

THE STRIPED SKUNK IS FOUND ALMOST EVERYWHERE IN CANADA AND IS EASILY IDENTIFIED BY ITS VIVID WHITE STRIPES. IT IS MOST ACTIVE AT NIGHT AND IS MORE OFTEN SMELLED THAN SEEN. THE SKUNK'S SCENT GLANDS, LOCATED AT THE BASE OF ITS TAIL, SHOOT A PUNGENT SPRAY AT ANYTHING THAT INSISTS ON GETTING TOO CLOSE — AS MANY COUNTRY SCHOOL CHILDREN AND THEIR DOGS HAVE DISCOVERED. BEFORE RESORTING TO ITS SPRAY, HOWEVER, THE SKUNK USUALLY GIVES FAIR WARNING BY RAISING THE HAIR ON ITS BACK, HISSING, AND STAMPING ITS FEET.

THE SKUNK'S HOME IS A BURROW, SOMETIMES FOUND UNDER BUILDINGS. FOUR TO TEN YOUNG ARE BORN IN EARLY SPRING AFTER A GESTATION PERIOD OF TWO MONTHS.

SKULL

THE SKUNK PREFERS TO DO ITS NOCTURNAL HUNTING IN MARSHLANDS, OPEN FIELDS, AND FOREST EDGES. IT EATS MICE, RATS, CHIPMUNKS, AND INSECTS, AS WELL AS FROGS, SNAKES, FRUIT, EGGS, AND CARRION. BECAUSE OF ITS NOCTURNAL INSTINCTS, ITS MOST FEARED ENEMY IS THE GREAT HORNED OWL.

SKUNKS MAKE AFFECTIONATE PETS, BUT, FOR AN OBVIOUS REASON, ONLY AFTER THE SCENT GLANDS HAVE BEEN REMOVED.

FRONT FOOT

HIND FOOT

OTTER

THE NORTH AMERICAN RIVER OTTER IS FOUND ON THE PACIFIC COAST AND IN RIVERS THROUGHOUT CANADA.

THIS FUN-LOVING MEMBER OF THE WEASEL FAMILY LIKES TO TUMBLE, WRESTLE, AND SLIDE DOWN CLAY OR SNOW BANKS. AN ADULT MALE OFTEN GROWS TO 1.2 M (4 FT.), INCLUDING ITS 50 CM (20 IN.) TAIL, AND CAN WEIGH UP TO 13 KG (30 LBS.). A SWIFT AND SKILLFUL SWIMMER, THE OTTER IS EASILY ABLE TO CATCH FISH, WHICH IS ITS MAIN FOOD SOURCE.

THE YOUNG, USUALLY TWO OR THREE, ARE BORN IN EARLY SPRING. THEY STAY CLOSE TO THEIR UNDERGROUND HOME, NOT VENTURING NEAR THE WATER UNTIL THEY ARE ABOUT TWO MONTHS OLD. THE YOUNG OTTERS STAY WITH THEIR MOTHER FOR ALMOST A YEAR, DURING WHICH TIME THEY RECEIVE A WELL-ROUNDED EDUCATION. THEY ARE TAUGHT TO SWIM AS EXPERTLY AS THEIR DAM, AND TO LIE QUIETLY UNDERWATER WITH ONLY NOSTRILS SHOWING WHEN DANGER APPEARS. NEXT, OF COURSE, COME THE FISHING LESSONS. THESE ARE GENEROUSLY LACED WITH FROLIC AND PLAY INVOLVING BOTH MOTHER AND YOUNG. IN LESS THAN A YEAR THE YOUNG OTTERS ARE READY TO TAKE THEIR PLACE IN THE HARSH WORLD OF NATURE.

THE SEA OTTER (NOT ILLUSTRATED) LIVES IN THE OCEAN WHERE IT FEEDS ON SEA URCHINS, CLAMS, AND FISH. IT IS A LARGER AND HEAVIER ANIMAL THAN THE RIVER OTTER WITH HIND FEET MODIFIED ALMOST TO FLIPPERS. ITS FUR HAS BEEN HIGHLY PRIZED BY TRADERS SINCE COOK FIRST LANDED AT NOOTKA IN 1778.

SEA OTTERS WERE SLAUGHTERED RUTHLESSLY BY FUR-TRADERS UNTIL NOT ONE ANIMAL REMAINED ALONG THE B.C. COAST. IN 1969, HOWEVER, 89 ALASKAN SEA OTTERS WERE RELEASED ON THE WEST COAST OF VANCOUVER ISLAND. THIS RELEASE AND OTHERS HAVE PROVED SUCCESSFUL AND TODAY THERE ARE OVER 300 OTTERS IN THE AREA. THEY ARE NOW PROTECTED BY LAW.

COUGAR

THE COUGAR, OR MOUNTAIN LION, IS SELDOM SEEN SINCE MOST OF ITS HUNTING IS DONE AT DUSK OR LATER. A LARGE COUGAR CAN MEASURE MORE THAN 2.7 M (9 FT.), INCLUDING A 76 CM (30 IN.) TAIL, AND WEIGH OVER 67 KG (150 LBS.). ITS COLOR IS REDDISH OR GREYISH AND IT CAN LIVE TWENTY YEARS OR SO.

THE BIG CAT'S FOOD CONSISTS MAINLY OF DEER, ALTHOUGH ELK, MOOSE, SHEEP, AND DOMESTIC STOCK ARE ALSO TAKEN. IT USUALLY FAVORS MOUNTAINOUS COUNTRY RATHER THAN GRASSLANDS OR PRAIRIES, AND PREFERS AN AREA WITH A LARGE DEER POPULATION. AS A CONSEQUENCE, IT IS SELDOM SEEN EAST OF THE ROCKIES.

THE COUGAR HAS NO PARTICULAR BREEDING PERIOD. AS A RESULT ONE TO FOUR YOUNG ARE BORN ANYTIME OF THE YEAR AFTER A GESTATION PERIOD OF NINETY DAYS. THE KITTENS' EYES OPEN AT NINE DAYS AND THEY ARE WEANED AND BEGIN TO EAT MEAT AT THREE MONTHS. THE YOUNG STAY WITH THEIR MOTHER FOR ONE TO TWO YEARS.

CANADA LYNX

THE CANADA LYNX IS FOUND THROUGHOUT CANADA EXCEPT ON THE WEST COAST AND PARTS OF MANITOBA. THE STAPLE FOOD OF THIS CAT IS THE VARYING, OR SNOWSHOE, HARE, THE LYNX POPULATION DEPENDING ALMOST ENTIRELY ON THE NUMBER OF HARES AVAILABLE.

THE CANADA LYNX, LIKE MOST MEMBERS OF THE CAT FAMILY IN THE WILD STATE, IS SELDOM SEEN. IT IS A CREATURE OF THE FOREST AND RARELY LEAVES THIS COVER, PARTICULARLY DURING DAYLIGHT HOURS. THE BOBCAT RESEMBLES THE LYNX BUT IS SMALLER AND HAS MORE CONSPICUOUS MARKINGS.

THE LYNX USUALLY WEIGHS ABOUT 9KG (20 LBS.) AND IS JUST UNDER 1M (3 FT.) LONG, INCLUDING ITS SHORT TAIL.

THE FEMALE BEARS ONE TO FOUR YOUNG APPROXIMATELY TWO MONTHS AFTER BREEDING, WHICH USUALLY TAKES PLACE IN FEBRUARY OR MARCH.

LIKE ALL CATS, THE LYNX EXPANDS OR CONTRACTS ITS PUPILS ACCORDING TO THE LIGHT AVAILABLE AND HAS RETRACTABLE CLAWS. IN ADDITION, IT HAS POWERFUL JAWS AND TEETH ADAPTED FOR TEARING AND CHEWING FLESH.

SEALS and SEA-LIONS

THE ELEPHANT AND HAIR SEALS BELONG TO A GROUP CALLED EARLESS SEALS, WHILE THE FUR SEAL AND SEA-LION ARE KNOWN AS EARED SEALS.

THE NORTHERN ELEPHANT SEAL, ALTHOUGH RARE IN B.C. WATERS, HAS BEEN SEEN ON OCCASION. IT IS A VERY LARGE SEAL – A BULL OFTEN ATTAINING 4.5 M (15 FT.) AND WEIGHING UP TO 1.8 TONNES (2 TONS). THE MALE IS EASILY RECOGNIZED BY ITS LARGE INFLATABLE SNOUT.

THE HAIR SEAL, OR HARBOUR SEAL, GROWS TO 1.5 M (5 FEET) AND SELDOM WEIGHS MORE THAN 135 KG (300 LBS.). THE BAYS AND INLETS OF B.C.'S COAST-LINE PLAY HOST TO THIS SEAL WHICH FEEDS ON FISH AND SHELLFISH.

ELEPHANT SEAL

HAIR SEAL

FUR SEAL

THE ADULT MALE FUR SEAL MAY WEIGH 270 KG (600 LBS.), WHILE THE FEMALE WEIGHS ONLY ABOUT 55 KG (120 LBS.). FEMALES AND YOUNG LEAVE THE PRIBILOF IS-LANDS IN LATE FALL AND TRAVEL SOUTH AS FAR AS CALIFORNIA, WHILE THE BULLS REMAIN IN NORTH-ERN WATERS.

A NORTHERN SEA-LION BULL MAY WEIGH MORE THAN 1 TONNE AND GROW TO OVER 3 M (10 FEET). THE FEMALE IS MUCH SMALLER, BUT STILL CAN WEIGH HALF A TONNE. DURING THE SUMMER THEY CAN BE FOUND ANYWHERE ALONG B.C.'S COAST.

SEA-LION

38

ELK

THE ELK, OR WAPITI, IS THE SECOND LARGEST MEMBER OF THE DEER FAMILY, THE MOOSE BEING THE LARGEST. A BULL ELK CAN WEIGH UP TO 45 KG (1,000 LBS.).

THE ELK LIVES ON MANY KINDS OF GRASSES, SHRUBS, AND TREES. ITS NATURAL ENEMIES ARE WOLVES, COUGARS, AND GRIZZLY BEARS. WHEN IT IS IN GOOD HEALTH WITH A FULL SET OF ANTLERS, HOWEVER, ITS ENEMIES ARE WISE TO LEAVE IT ALONE. WINTER STARVATION AND PARASITIC DISEASES TAKE THE LARGEST TOLL OF ELK.

ELK HERDS SPEND THEIR WINTERS IN PROTECTED TREE-LINED VALLEYS. IN SUMMER THEY MOVE UP TO TIMBERLINE.

IN EARLY FALL WHEN MATING SEASON STARTS, A BULL MAY GATHER A HAREM OF TWENTY OR MORE. IT THEN FACES THE TASK OF PROTECTING ITS HAREM FROM OTHER BULLS. SOMETIMES A YOUNG BULL DECIDES TO TEST AN OLDER BULL'S ABILITY AND A GREAT SHOVING AND GRUNTING MATCH ENSUES, OFTEN LASTING FOR HOURS.

THE DRAWINGS BELOW ILLUSTRATE THE ELK'S ANTLER GROWTH. THE ANTLERS ARE SHED IN MARCH.

IN LATE APRIL THE NEW ANTLERS BEGIN TO APPEAR AS FUZZY KNOBS.

IN JUNE THE GROWING ANTLERS ARE STILL SOFT.

IN AUGUST THE ANTLERS BECOME HARD AND THE ELK RUBS THEM ON TREE TRUNKS TO REMOVE THE VELVET-LIKE SKIN.

DEER

BOTH THE MULE AND THE WHITETAIL DEER ARE FOUND IN WESTERN CANADA, WHILE THE COLUMBIA BLACKTAIL DEER INHABITS ONLY THE PACIFIC COAST AND ITS ISLANDS.

THE MULE DEER, ABOVE, BROWSES ON A VARIETY OF TREES, INCLUDING ASPEN AND WILLOW. IT ALSO EATS GRASS AND, WHEN FOOD IS SCARCE, WILL EVEN BROWSE ON FIR TREES.

THE COLUMBIA BLACKTAIL (NOT ILLUSTRATED) IS A SMALLER RELATIVE OF THE MULE DEER AND SIMILAR IN APPEARANCE. LIKE THE MULE DEER, ITS ANTLERS GROW IN FORKED FORMATION RATHER THAN AS POINTS FROM A MAIN BRANCH SUCH AS THE WHITETAIL'S.

THE WHITETAIL IS EASILY RECOGNIZED, PARTICULARLY WHEN IT IS RUNNING, BY THE WHITE UNDERSIDE OF ITS LARGE TAIL. THE WHITETAIL HAS BEEN KNOWN TO RUN NEARLY 60 KPH (40 MPH), JUMP WINDFALLS 2.5 M (8 FT.) HIGH, AND COVER 9M (30 FT.) IN A SINGLE BOUND.

THE MAIN CAUSES OF DEATH AMONG DEER, ASIDE FROM HUNTERS AND PREDATORS, ARE WINTER STARVATION AND PARASITIC DISEASES.

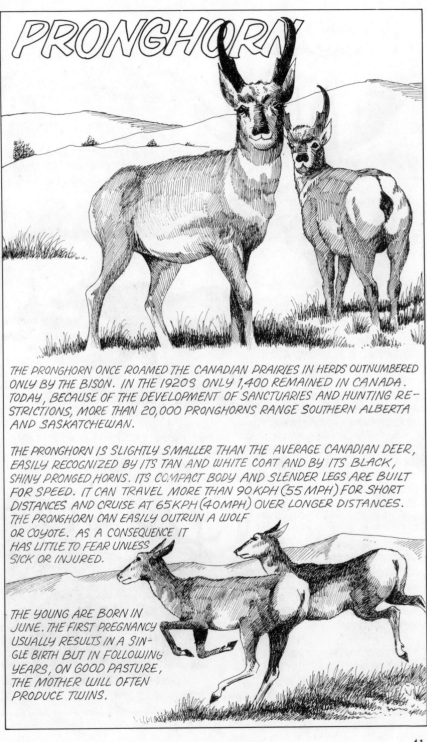

PRONGHORN

THE PRONGHORN ONCE ROAMED THE CANADIAN PRAIRIES IN HERDS OUTNUMBERED ONLY BY THE BISON. IN THE 1920S ONLY 1,400 REMAINED IN CANADA. TODAY, BECAUSE OF THE DEVELOPMENT OF SANCTUARIES AND HUNTING RESTRICTIONS, MORE THAN 20,000 PRONGHORNS RANGE SOUTHERN ALBERTA AND SASKATCHEWAN.

THE PRONGHORN IS SLIGHTLY SMALLER THAN THE AVERAGE CANADIAN DEER, EASILY RECOGNIZED BY ITS TAN AND WHITE COAT AND BY ITS BLACK, SHINY PRONGED HORNS. ITS COMPACT BODY AND SLENDER LEGS ARE BUILT FOR SPEED. IT CAN TRAVEL MORE THAN 90 KPH (55 MPH) FOR SHORT DISTANCES AND CRUISE AT 65 KPH (40 MPH) OVER LONGER DISTANCES. THE PRONGHORN CAN EASILY OUTRUN A WOLF OR COYOTE. AS A CONSEQUENCE IT HAS LITTLE TO FEAR UNLESS SICK OR INJURED.

THE YOUNG ARE BORN IN JUNE. THE FIRST PREGNANCY USUALLY RESULTS IN A SINGLE BIRTH BUT IN FOLLOWING YEARS, ON GOOD PASTURE, THE MOTHER WILL OFTEN PRODUCE TWINS.

MOOSE

PERHAPS THE MOST IMPRESSIVE FEATURE OF THE MOOSE IS ITS MAGNIFICENT RACK OF ANTLERS WHICH CAN SPAN 190 CM (75 IN.). THE ADULT BULL SHEDS ITS ANTLERS IN DECEMBER OR JANUARY AND GROWS A NEW SET BEFORE THE MATING SEASON IN SEPTEMBER. THE BULL MOOSE DOES NOT COLLECT A HAREM IN THE MANNER OF AN ELK, BUT PREFERS TO MOVE FROM ONE COW TO ANOTHER.

SINCE THE MOOSE'S SHORT NECK MAKES IT UNSUITED FOR GRAZING, IT IS A BROWSER. ITS PREFERENCE RUNS TO WILLOW, ASPEN, AND BIRCH, AS WELL AS MANY AQUATIC PLANTS FROM LAKE BOTTOMS. IN SUMMER, IN FACT, MUCH OF THE MOOSE'S TIME IS SPENT IN THE WATER. IT IS AN EXCELLENT SWIMMER, EASILY COVERING 25 OR 30 KM (15 OR 20 MILES). IN ADDITION, IT IS A POWERFUL TRAVELER ON LAND AND CAN TROT HOUR AFTER HOUR. DURING THE RUTTING SEASON THE BULL MOOSE IS ONE OF THE MOST DANGEROUS ANIMALS IN THE WOODS, EVEN KNOWN TO ATTACK VEHICLES AND TRAINS.

CALVES ARE BORN EARLY IN JUNE. THEY WEIGH 13 TO 17 KG (30 TO 40 LBS.) AT BIRTH, ARE FLAT BROWN IN COLOR, AND LACK THE SPOTS USUALLY FOUND ON YOUNG MEMBERS OF THE DEER FAMILY.

EVEN GRIZZLY BEARS AND WOLF PACKS HESITATE TO ATTACK THIS LARGEST MEMBER OF THE DEER FAMILY.

CARIBOU

THE MAGNIFICENTLY ANTLERED CARIBOU IS AN INHABITANT OF NORTHERN CANADA. IT IS STILL OF ECONOMIC IMPORTANCE TO NATIVE PEOPLE BUT NOT LIKE IN BYGONE DAYS WHEN THEY DEPENDED ALMOST ENTIRELY ON THE ANIMAL FOR FOOD AND CLOTHING. NO ATTEMPTS TO DOMESTICATE THE CARIBOU HAVE BEEN MADE IN CANADA.

A HAREM OF TWELVE TO FIFTEEN COWS IS MAINTAINED BY A SINGLE BULL WHICH MUST FREQUENTLY BATTLE TO PROTECT ITS COWS FROM RIVALS.

THE SPLENDID ANTLERS OF THE CARIBOU ARE MUCH SOUGHT AFTER BY BIG-GAME HUNTERS. THE FIRST TINE ON ONE OF THE ANTLERS IS PALMATED AND EXTENDS OVER THE FACE TO FORM WHAT IS CALLED A PLOUGH, OR A SHOVEL. THE CARIBOU IS THE ONLY MEMBER OF THE DEER FAMILY IN WHICH BOTH MALE AND FEMALE CARRY ANTLERS. THE BULL SHEDS ITS DURING WINTER WHILE THE COW SHEDS AFTER CALVING, USUALLY LATE IN MAY.

A CALF HAS A SOLID LIGHT BROWN PELAGE AND USUALLY WEIGHS ABOUT 3.5 KG (8 LBS.) AT BIRTH. IT IS WEANED IN THE EARLY FALL BUT STAYS WITH ITS MOTHER UNTIL THE AUTUMN OF THE FOLLOWING YEAR. A COW GENERALLY REARS ABOUT SIX CALVES DURING ITS LIFETIME.

BISON

PLAINS BISON ONCE INHABITED MOST OF THE AREA NOW KNOWN AS THE PRAIRIE PROVINCES, WHILE WOOD BISON ROAMED THE NORTHEAST CORNER OF B.C., THE YUKON, AND PART OF THE NORTHWEST TERRITORIES. THE WOODS BISON IS LARGER AND DARKER THAN THE PLAINS BISON. THERE ARE AT PRESENT SEVERAL CONTROLLED HERDS OF BOTH WOOD AND PLAINS BISON IN WESTERN CANADA.

THE PLAINS BISON PROBABLY PENETRATED B.C.'S EASTERN BORDER BY WAY OF THE ROCKY MOUNTAIN'S ALPINE MEADOWS.

A FULLY GROWN BULL CAN BE 3.5 M (12 FT.) LONG, STAND 2 M (6 FT.) HIGH, AND WEIGH UP TO 1 TONNE. THE COWS ARE SMALLER, SOME 1.5 M (5 FT.) AT THE SHOULDER AND WEIGH ABOUT 405 KG (900 LBS.). THE HORNS OF A LARGE BULL CAN BE OVER .5 M (2 FT.) LONG WITH A BASE CIRCUMFERENCE OF 39 CM (16 IN.).

THE CALVES STAY WITH THE COWS FOR THREE YEARS UNTIL READY FOR BREEDING. COWS MAY BEAR CALVES EVERY YEAR FOR TWENTY YEARS.

MUSK-OX

THE MUSK-OX RANGES ACROSS NORTHERN CANADA FROM HUDSON BAY TO THE YUKON AND, UNLIKE THE CARIBOU, DOES NOT MIGRATE SOUTH NO MATTER HOW HARSH THE WINTER. THE MUSK-OX IS WELL INSULATED IN THICK WOOL WHICH IS COVERED BY A COAT OF SILKEN HAIR LONGER THAN THE BODY HAIR OF ANY OTHER ANIMAL.

A FULL GROWN BULL STANDS BETWEEN 1.2 AND 1.5 M (4 AND 5 FT.) AND WEIGHS BETWEEN 230 AND 360 KG (500 AND 800 LBS.). A COW IS CONSIDERABLY SMALLER.

THE SHORT NORTHERN SUMMER PROVIDES THE MUSK-OX WITH A VARIETY OF FORAGE. IN WINTER IT PAWS THROUGH THE SNOW TO FEED, MOVING FROM AREA TO AREA WHEREVER THE SNOW IS LIGHTEST.

WHEN THREATENED, THE MUSK-OX IS NOT THE TIMID OR PASSIVE BEAST IT APPEARS TO BE, BUT A TOUGH OPPONENT CAPABLE OF ROUTING ITS ENEMIES. WHEN A HERD IS ATTACKED BY A PACK OF WOLVES, THE BULLS AND COWS FORM A CIRCLE WITH THEIR HORNS TOWARD THE ENEMY, THE CALVES SAFE IN THE CENTER.

MOUNTAIN GOAT

WESTERN CANADA'S WORLD FAMOUS MOUNTAIN GOAT IS NOT REALLY A GOAT AT ALL, BUT A MEMBER OF THE ANTELOPE FAMILY. IT MAKES ITS HOME WELL ABOVE TIMBERLINE ON THE LARGER MOUNTAIN RANGES THROUGHOUT THE WEST, ALTHOUGH SEVERE WINTERS OFTEN DRIVE IT TO THE LOWER VALLEYS. BECAUSE OF THE SHORTAGE OF FORAGE IN ITS HABITAT, THE MOUNTAIN GOAT IS QUITE WILLING TO EAT ALMOST ANYTHING THAT IS GREENISH IN COLOR.

THE MALE USUALLY TRAVELS ALONE BUT SOMETIMES TWO OR THREE MAY BE OBSERVED TOGETHER. BREEDING TAKES PLACE IN EARLY WINTER, WITH THE YOUNG BORN SIX MONTHS LATER. WHILE WOLVES AND BEARS PREY ON THE YOUNG, WHEN THE GOATS REACH MATURITY THEIR MAIN HAZARDS ARE FALLS AND AVALANCHES, AND MAN WITH HIS HIGHPOWERED WEAPONS.

THE MOUNTAIN GOAT'S HOOVES ARE CUSHIONED WITH RUBBER-LIKE PADS THAT PROVIDE A POSITIVE GRIP ON ROCKY SURFACES. THEY ARE THE MAJOR REASON IT IS ABLE TO MAKE ASTONISHING LEAPS FROM ONE TINY LEDGE TO ANOTHER.

FRONT—

HIND—

THE HORN SHEATHS ARE MISSING FROM THE SKULL SHOWN HERE. THE POINTS OF THE HOOF ARE QUITE NARROW AND TEND TO SPREAD. THE TRACKS SHOWN ARE WALKING TRACKS.

BIGHORN

THE ROCKY MOUNTAIN BIGHORN SPENDS THE SUMMER FEEDING ON HIGH MOUNTAIN PASTURES AND THE WINTER FORAGING AT LOWER LEVELS. THE BIGHORN CAN SURVIVE FOR LONG PERIODS OF TIME ON VERY LITTLE VEGETATION BUT MUST HAVE DAILY ACCESS TO WATER AND PERIODIC ACCESS TO SALT. BECAUSE IT HAS A POOR SENSE OF SMELL, ITS SAFETY DEPENDS GREATLY ON ITS EXCEPTIONAL SIGHT.

BREEDING TAKES PLACE IN EARLY WINTER AND THE YOUNG, OFTEN TWINS IN GOOD PASTURE AREAS, ARE BORN AFTER A GESTATION PERIOD OF APPROXIMATELY SIX MONTHS. IN EARLY SPRING THE RAMS BAND TOGETHER AND INHABIT SEPARATE PASTURES FROM THE EWES AND YOUNG.

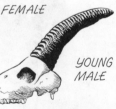

FEMALE

YOUNG MALE

OLD MALE

THE DISTINCTIVE HORNS OF THIS SHEEP ARE MUCH SOUGHT AFTER BY TROPHY HUNTERS. THE HORNS ARE MASSIVE IN CONSTRUCTION, BROWN IN COLOR, AND MARKED WITH GROWTH RINGS. THE HORNS OF THE FEMALE CLOSELY RESEMBLE THOSE OF THE FARMYARD NANNY GOAT.

STONE SHEEP

STONE SHEEP INHABIT THE NORTHERN PART OF BRITISH COLUMBIA AND MOST OF THE YUKON. RAMS TRAVEL IN BANDS OF TEN OR TWENTY BUT EWES AND LAMBS FORM MUCH LARGER BANDS.

THE STONE SHEEP'S FOOD IS ALMOST EXCLUSIVELY GRASS, AND IT CAN GO WITHOUT WATER FOR TWO OR THREE DAYS.

IN NOVEMBER THE RAMS BATTLE FOR POSSESSION OF A FEW EWES AND IN MAY THE LAMBS ARE BORN IN A SECLUDED, SHELTERED PLACE. AFTER A WEEK OR TWO OF SOLITUDE MOTHER AND OFFSPRING JOIN THE MAIN HERD.

THIS SHEEP RANGES IN COLOR FROM ALMOST WHITE TO BLACK, WITH ALL SHADES OF BROWN OR BLUE-GREY IN BETWEEN.

LOONS

THE SWIMMING ABILITY OF THE LOON IS EXTRAORDINARY – WHEN FISHING IT CAN DIVE TO 53 M (175 FT.) AND REMAIN UNDERWATER FOR TEN MINUTES OR MORE. THE SCREAMS AND CRAZY LAUGHTER-LIKE CALL OF A LOON AT NIGHT ARE QUITE APT TO CHILL THE BLOOD OF THOSE NOT FAMILIAR WITH THESE OUTBURSTS. THERE ARE SEVERAL SPECIES OF LOONS, SHOWN HERE IN SUMMER PLUMAGE.

THE COMMON LOON, LEFT, LIKE ALL LOONS, LOSES ITS FANCY PATTERNS IN WINTER AND BECOMES QUITE DRAB. ITS WINTERS ARE SPENT ON SALT WATER, ITS SUMMERS ON INLAND LAKES.

THE YELLOW-BILLED LOON, RIGHT, IS NOT UNLIKE THE COMMON LOON BUT IS A LITTLE LARGER AND HAS A CONSPICUOUS YELLOW BILL.

THE ARCTIC LOON, BELOW, ALSO KNOWN AS THE BLACK-THROATED LOON, IS MUCH SMALLER THAN OTHER LOONS.

THE RED-THROATED LOON, BELOW, IS A WIDE-RANGING BIRD FOUND IN NORTHERN AREAS FROM NEWFOUNDLAND TO B.C. UNLIKE ITS RELATIVES, IT FLIES RATHER THAN DIVES WHEN IT FEELS THE NEED TO ESCAPE FROM INTRUDERS.

THE LEGS OF A LOON ARE SO FAR BACK ON ITS BODY THAT IT FINDS WALKING ON LAND ALMOST IMPOSSIBLE. FOR THIS REASON IT NESTS NEAR WATER'S EDGE, USUALLY IN A DEPRESSION WHICH HOLDS A PAIR OF OLIVE-COLORED EGGS THAT ARE GENEROUSLY SPOTTED WITH BROWN.

LOONS DINE CHIEFLY ON SHELLFISH, CRUSTACEANS, SMALL FISH, AND A VARIETY OF VEGETATION.

CORMORANTS

THREE SPECIES OF THE CORMORANT FAMILY INHABIT B.C.'S WEST COAST THROUGHOUT THE YEAR. ALL ARE SIMILAR IN APPEARANCE AND HABIT. THEY NEST IN COLONIES HIGH ON ROCKY LEDGES AND OFTEN SHARE THE NESTING SITE WITH OTHER VARIETIES OF SEA BIRDS. THE CORMORANT'S NATURAL ENEMY IS THE WESTERN GULL, WHICH FEEDS ON ITS EGGS AND THE YOUNG CORMORANTS.

THIS LARGE SEA BIRD IS 60 TO 90CM (25 TO 35 IN.) IN LENGTH AND USUALLY WEIGHS 1.5 TO 2 KG (3 TO 4 LBS.). IT IS GENERALLY BLACK IN COLOR WITH TOUCHES OF GREEN AND PURPLE IRIDESCENCE.

THE CORMORANT LIVES ALMOST EXCLUSIVELY ON FISH. CONSEQUENTLY, IT IS AN EXPERT DIVER AND SWIMMER. DIVES TO MORE THAN 60 M (200 FT.) HAVE BEEN RECORDED. FOLLOWING AN UNDERWATER FISHING SESSION, THE CORMORANT IS OFTEN SEEN PERCHED ON A ROCK OR LOG WITH WINGS EXTENDED FOR DRYING.

GREAT BLUE HERON

THE TALL, LONG-LEGGED, LONG-NECKED
BLUE HERON IS A COMMON SUMMER VISITOR
TO WESTERN CANADA. IT IS OFTEN SEEN ON INLAND
LAKES AND MARSHES, AS WELL AS COASTAL BAYS AND INLETS.
MANY REMAIN IN SOUTHERN BRITISH COLUMBIA THROUGHOUT THE WINTER.

THIS HERON'S NEST, CONSTRUCTED OF STICKS AND TWIGS, IS BUILT HIGH IN AN
OLD TREE, USUALLY CLOSE TO WATER AND IN A COLONY. OCCASIONALLY,
HOWEVER, A NEST CAN BE FOUND IN LOW SHRUBBERY OR ON THE GROUND.

THE GREAT BLUE HERON STANDS AP-
PROXIMATELY 1.25 M (4 FT.) HIGH, ITS
WINGSPREAD SOMETIMES EXEEDING 1.8 M
(6 FT.). ITS COLOR IS SLATE BLUE WITH
A BLACK AND WHITE HEAD AND A CHEST-
NUT PATCH ON EACH SHOULDER. ITS
BILL IS BLACK AND YELLOW, ABOUT
15 CM (6 IN.) LONG AND VERY SHARP.

THE HERON IS OFTEN SEEN WADING MA-
JESTICALLY THROUGH SHALLOW WATERS AT
A SLOW DELIBERATE PACE, HEAD TURN-
ING FROM SIDE TO SIDE, RAZOR-SHARP
BILL POISED TO STRIKE AN UNWARY PREY.

THE SPECIES DINES MAINLY ON FISH, FROGS,
SNAKES, EELS, SALAMANDERS AND ASS-
ORTED INSECTS.

TRUMPETER SWAN

THE TRUMPETER SWAN IS CANADA'S LARGEST WATERFOWL. IT CAN WEIGH UP TO 9 KG (20 LBS.) AND MEASURE ALMOST 2M (6 FT.) FROM BILL TO TAIL.

ALTHOUGH THE TRUMPETER IS FAIRLY CLOSE TO EXTINCTION, SEVERAL THOUSAND STILL SURVIVE. IT BREEDS IN NORTHERN ALBERTA AND BRITISH COLUMBIA AND, IF THE WEATHER ISN'T TOO SEVERE, SPENDS WINTERS IN PARTS OF INTERIOR AND COASTAL B.C.

THIS LARGE BIRD FEEDS MAINLY ON THE LEAVES, ROOTS, AND SEEDS OF AQUATIC PLANTS. THE FEMALE LAYS SIX OR SEVEN LARGE WHITE EGGS. THE YOUNG TRUMPETER WEARS A COAT OF GREY DURING ITS FIRST YEAR AND USUALLY ACQUIRES THE WHITE PLUMAGE OF AN ADULT IN ITS SECOND OR THIRD YEAR.

THE TRUMPETER SWAN IS SIMILAR IN APPEARANCE TO THE WHISTLING SWAN, ALTHOUGH THE WHISTLER IS CONSIDERABLY SMALLER AND HAS YELLOW SPOTS AT THE BASE OF ITS BILL. THE TRUMPETER DOES NOT SCARE EASILY. THIS TRAIT MAY BE RESPONSIBLE FOR ITS NEAR DEMISE.

CANADA GOOSE

FOUR SPECIES OF CANADA GOOSE INHABIT DIFFERENT PARTS OF CANADA AND AT DIFFERENT TIMES OF THE YEAR. THEY ARE THE HONKER, THE WESTERN, THE CACKLING, AND THE LESSER. ALL ARE SIMILAR EXCEPT IN SIZE AND COLOR.

THIS LARGE BIRD USES A V-FORMATION IN MIGRATORY FLIGHT AND CRUISES AT SPEEDS FROM 32 KMH (20 MPH) TO 72 KMH (45 MPH).

THE CANADA FEEDS MAINLY ON AQUATIC PLANTS, GRASS, AND GRAIN WHEN AVAILABLE.

THE NEST IS USUALLY BUILT ON THE GROUND CLOSE TO WATER. THE FEMALE LAYS AND INCUBATES FOUR TO SIX OLIVE COLORED EGGS. CANADAS ARE FIERCELY PROTECTIVE PARENTS AND WILL ATTACK VICIOUSLY ANY INTRUDER.

SNOW GOOSE

THE LESSER SNOW, COMMONLY KNOWN AS THE "WAVIE," IS A MUCH SMALLER BIRD THAN THE CANADA. ITS PLUMAGE IS WHITE EXCEPT FOR BLACK WING TIPS. IN CANADA THIS BIRD IS FOUND ONLY IN WINTER ON THE SOUTH COAST OF B.C. A MUCH SMALLER SPECIES IS THE ROSS GOOSE WHICH IS SELDOM SEEN IN CANADA.

THE SNOW GOOSE, WHICH AVERAGES ABOUT 2 KG (4 LBS.), FEEDS ON MUCH THE SAME FOOD AS THE CANADA, BUT SINCE IT WINTERS EXCLUSIVELY ON THE COAST, LITTLE GRAIN IS INCLUDED IN ITS DIET.

NESTING HABITS ARE SIMILAR TO THOSE OF THE CANADA. THE YOUNG GROW RAPIDLY BUT THEIR PLUMAGE REMAINS GREY UNTIL THE FOLLOWING SUMMER WHEN THEY ATTAIN THE WHITE AND BLACK PLUMAGE OF THE ADULT.

MALLARD

AS WELL AS BEING CANADA'S MOST PLENTI-
FUL DUCK, THE MALLARD IS THE ANCESTOR
OF MANY DOMESTIC DUCKS. IT IS FOUND
ALMOST EVERYWHERE IN NORTH AMERICA
EXCEPT FOR THE EXTREME NORTH AND
SOUTH.

THE MALE MALLARD IS A LARGE HAND-
SOME DUCK. AN IRIDESCENT GREEN HEAD
AND A WHITE RING AROUND THE NECK ARE
ITS IDENTIFICATION MARKS. THE
FEMALE IS A MOTTLED BUFF AND
BROWN AND LOOKS A GREAT DEAL
LIKE THE HEN OF OTHER SPECIES.
THE DRAKE MOULTS EVERY
SUMMER, ITS NEW PLU-
MAGE MUCH THE SAME AS
THE FEMALE'S. IN THE FALL
IT MOULTS AGAIN, THIS
TIME EXCHANGING ITS
HEN-LIKE FEATHERS FOR
FANCY BREEDING PLUMAGE.
THE AVERAGE DRAKE
WEIGHS 1.3K (3 LBS.);
THE FEMALE, A
LITTLE LESS.

THE MALLARD FEEDS MAINLY ON AQUATIC
VEGETATION, GRAINS, SEEDS, AND NUTS WHEN-
EVER AVAILABLE. IT IS ALSO FOND OF APPLES,
POTATOES, AND CORN.

THE MALLARD USUALLY NESTS ON THE
GROUND, ALTHOUGH IT SOMETIMES PREFERS
HOLLOW STUMPS OR BRUSH, OFTEN FAR FROM
WATER. THE HEN FILLS THE NEST WITH ABOUT
TEN EGGS, COVERS THEM WITH DOWN
FROM HER BREAST, THEN INCUBATES
ABOUT TWENTY-SIX DAYS. YOUNG
ARE RAISED EXCLUSIVELY BY THE
HEN, THE DRAKE HAVING GONE OFF
ON HIS OWN TO MOULT.

ECONOMICALLY, THE MALLARD IS
ONE OF MAN'S MOST VALUABLE BIRDS,
FOR CENTURIES SUPPLYING FOOD
AND STILL TODAY AN IMPORTANT
GAME BIRD.

PINTAIL

THE PINTAIL'S MOST RECOGNIZABLE FEATURES ARE ITS LONG POINTED TAIL AND SLENDER NECK. THE FEMALE DOES NOT HAVE A POINTED TAIL BUT CLOSELY RESEMBLES THE FEMALE MALLARD IN APPEARANCE. THE PINTAIL PREFERS FRESH WATER AND, SINCE IT IS A SURFACE FEEDER, SELDOM DIVES. ANOTHER OF ITS CHARACTERISTICS IS THAT WHEN TAKING OFF FROM WATER, IT DOES NOT FLY ALONG THE SURFACE BUT RISES, ROCKET-LIKE, ALMOST STRAIGHT UP.

ITS FOOD CONSISTS MAINLY OF WATER PLANTS AND SEEDS, WITH SOME INSECTS AND MOLLUSKS. THE HEN USUALLY BUILDS ITS NEST ON DRY GROUND, OFTEN A FAIR DISTANCE FROM THE WATER. THE NEST MAY CONTAIN UP TO TEN PALE OLIVE EGGS.

THE PINTAIL INHABITS ALL OF CANADA DURING THE SUMMER. IN AUGUST IT STARTS HEADING FOR WINTERING GROUNDS IN THE SOUTHERN UNITED STATES, MEXICO, AND CENTRAL AMERICA. AS A GAME BIRD, IT IS ALMOST AS POPULAR AS THE MALLARD.

TEAL

THE GREEN-WINGED TEAL IS EASILY IDENTIFIED BY ITS RED HEAD AND GREEN EYE PATCH, AS WELL AS WHITE CRESCENTS ON ITS SHOULDERS. IT OFTEN TRAVELS IN LARGE FLOCKS AT HIGH SPEEDS, TWISTING AND TURNING WITH REMARKABLE PRECISION. PLANTS MAKE UP THE MAIN PART OF THIS DUCK'S DIET, WITH SEEDS BEING ITS FAVORITE. MOLLUSKS AND INSECTS ARE ALSO EATEN WHEN AVAILABLE. THE AVERAGE GREEN-WINGED TEAL WEIGHS 700 G (13 OZ.).

THE BLUE-WINGED TEAL IS READILY IDENTIFIED BY ITS DARK HEAD AND WHITE CRESCENTS IN FRONT OF ITS EYES. THIS DUCK IS FOUND THROUGHOUT THE PRAIRIES AND IN BRITISH COLUMBIA'S INTERIOR. WHEN IN FLIGHT IT CRUISES AT SPEEDS BETWEEN 50 KPH (30 MPH) AND 60 KPH (36 MPH). WHEN PURSUED IT CAN ATTAIN EVEN HIGHER SPEEDS. THE BLUE-WINGED TEAL MIGRATES FURTHER SOUTH THAN ANY OTHER NORTH AMERICAN DUCK.

THE CINNAMON TEAL CANNOT BE MISTAKEN FOR ANY OTHER TEAL BECAUSE OF ITS CINNAMON-RED HEAD AND BODY. IT IS SEEN ONLY IN THE AREA WEST OF THE ROCKY MOUNTAINS, WITH SOUTHERN BRITISH COLUMBIA THE LIMIT OF ITS NORTHERN RANGE.

THE DIETS AND MATING HABITS OF ALL TEAL ARE SIMILAR. WHILE THE DRAKES ARE READILY IDENTIFIED, THE HENS ARE A PROBLEM BECAUSE THEY ARE ALMOST IDENTICAL TO ONE ANOTHER. THEY ARE, OF COURSE, MUCH DRABBER THAN THE DRAKES. THE TEAL FAMILY IS A FAVORITE WITH SPORTSMEN. THE BIRDS ARE FAST, PLUMP AND, BECAUSE THEY FEED MAINLY ON VEGETATION, QUITE PALATABLE.

WOOD DUCK

THE WOOD DUCK BREEDS IN SOUTH-
ERN BRITISH COLUMBIA AND SOUTHERN
MANITOBA, AS WELL AS IN SOME OF
THE EASTERN PROVINCES. IT PRE-
FERS AREAS WITH STILL, FRESH
WATER SURROUNDED BY TREES.
A BEAUTIFULLY COLORED BIRD, IT
BECOMES QUITE TAME IF UNMOLEST-
ED. THE WOOD DUCK DINES LARGELY
ON VEGETABLE MATTER SUCH AS
DUCKWEED, SEEDS, NUTS, AND THE
OCCASIONAL INSECT.

THE WOOD DUCK'S NEST
IS USUALLY FOUND IN A HOL-
LOW OF AN OLD TREE TRUNK,
NOT NECESSARILY CLOSE TO
WATER. IT MAY BE NEAR
GROUND LEVEL OR MORE THAN
20 M (65 FT.) HIGH. APPROXIMATELY
TWELVE BUFF EGGS HATCH IN THE SPRING.

THE HANDSOME MALE WOOD DUCK IS EASILY IDEN-
TIFIED BY ITS IRIDESCENT BLUE-GREEN HEAD
AND BACK, WHITE MARKINGS ON THE SIDES OF
ITS HEAD, AND RICH MAHOGANY-RED CHEST SPOTTED WITH WHITE.
THE WOOD DUCK WINTERS FROM SOUTHERN CANADA TO MEXICO.

REDHEAD

THE REDHEAD DUCK IS FOUND MAINLY IN THE PRAIRIE PROVINCES, ALTHOUGH IT IS SOMETIMES SEEN IN SMALL NUMBERS IN THE B. C. INTERIOR. AS ITS NAME INDICATES, THIS DUCK HAS A RED HEAD. ITS BREAST IS BLACK, ITS BACK LIGHT GREY AND ITS BELLY WHITE. THE HEN IS VARIOUS SHADES OF BROWN.

THE RED HEAD IS A DIVING DUCK BUT, UNLIKE MOST DIVING DUCKS, FEEDS ALMOST ENTIRELY ON VEGETABLE MATTER.

ITS NEST, USUALLY IN A MARSH, IS CAREFULLY CONSTRUCTED AND LINED WITH DOWN. WHEN THE FIVE TO TWELVE EGGS ARE LAID THEY ALSO ARE COVERED WITH DOWN.

ONCE ONE OF THE MOST COMMON DUCKS IN CANADA, THE REDHEAD POPULATION HAS BEEN GREATLY REDUCED BY CULTIVATION OF ITS ORIGINAL NESTING GROUNDS, NOW THE VAST WHEAT FIELDS OF CANADA AND THE UNITED STATES.

CANVAS-BACK

THE CANVAS-BACK IS ONE OF OUR LARGER DIVING DUCKS. IT IS FOUND IN LARGE NUMBERS IN WESTERN CANADA DURING THE SUMMER MONTHS. IN WINTER IT IS QUITE COMMON ON B.C.'S SOUTH COAST. THE CANVAS-BACK'S PLUMAGE IS ALMOST THE SAME AS THAT OF THE RED-HEAD DUCK. IT HAS A RED HEAD AND NECK, CANVAS-COLORED BACK, AND BLACK BREAST AND SHOULDERS.

THE CANVAS-BACK'S NEST IS USUALLY WELL HIDDEN AND CLOSE TO THE WATER'S EDGE. THE EGGS, APPROXIMATELY EIGHT TO A SETTING, ARE DARK OLIVE IN COLOR. AS SOON AS THEY ARE ALL LAID THE MALE LEAVES THE FEMALE.

THIS SPECIES OF DUCK IS A FAVORITE OF DUCK HUNTERS SINCE ITS MEAT IS QUITE PALATABLE AND IT IS A FAST FLIER.

GOLDENEYE

THE GOLDENEYE INHABITS ALL OF WESTERN CANADA AT VARIOUS TIMES OF THE YEAR. IT MIGRATES TO THE B.C. COAST IN LATE FALL AND THEN HEADS SOUTH FOR THE WINTER. THE DRAKE IS EASILY IDENTIFIED BY ITS STRIKING BLACK AND WHITE PLUMAGE AND WHITE FACE PATCHES. THE HEN IS PREDOMINANTLY GREY WITH A RICH BROWN HEAD.

AMERICAN GOLDENEYE

THIS DUCK USUALLY NESTS IN A TREE, UTILIZING AN ABANDONED WOODPECKER'S HOLE OR SOME OTHER CAVITY. THE EGGS ARE GREEN IN COLOR AND NUMBER SIX TO EIGHTEEN. BY JUNE THE DUCKLINGS ARE ABLE TO SWIM WITH THEIR MOTHER.

THE GOLDENEYE EATS MOSTLY ANIMAL MATTER SUCH AS INSECTS, MOLLUSKS, AND CRUSTACEANS. THIS PREFERENCE FOR ANIMAL FOOD MAKES THE GOLDENEYE CONSIDERABLY LESS PALATABLE THAN THE GRAIN-EATING DUCKS. NEVERTHELESS, IT IS POPULAR WITH DUCK HUNTERS BECAUSE OF ITS SWIFT AND ERRATIC FLIGHT.

BARROW GOLDENEYE

61

MERGANSERS

THE RED-BREASTED MERGANSER, CENTER, LIKE THE OTHER MERGANSERS, HAS A LONG ROUND BILL WITH TEETH FOR CATCHING AND HOLDING FISH. THIS BIRD PREFERS SALT WATER AND ALWAYS NESTS UPON THE GROUND. EIGHT TO TEN EGGS ARE LAID IN A DOWN-LINED NEST. UNLIKE OTHER MERGANSERS, THE MALE OF THIS SPECIES ASSISTS THE FEMALE IN REARING THE YOUNG. IDENTIFICATION IS FACILITATED BY THE HAIRY CREST ON THE BIRD'S HEAD.

PERHAPS THE MOST EASILY IDENTIFIED OF THE MERGANSERS IS THE HOODED MERGANSER, LEFT. IT PREFERS THE QUIET OF WOODED PONDS OR STREAMS TO SALT WATER. FISHERMEN SHOULDN'T OBJECT TO THIS BIRD BECAUSE IT IS NOT A CONFIRMED FISH-EATER. THE FEMALE USUALLY LAYS NINE OR MORE EGGS IN A HOLLOW TREE AND AFTER THIRTY-ONE DAYS OF INCUBATION THE EGGS ARE HATCHED.

THE AMERICAN, OR COMMON, MERGANSER, IS THE LARGEST OF THE THREE MERGANSERS NATIVE TO CANADA. ITS NEST MAY BE ON THE GROUND, IN HOLLOW TREES, OR ON CLIFFS. LIKE THE OTHER MERGANSERS, IT LIVES ON FISH, ROE, CRUSTACEANS, AND SOME INSECTS. THE MAJORITY OF ITS FOOD IS OBTAINED BY DIVING, AN ACTIVITY TO WHICH ITS STREAMLINED BODY IS WELL SUITED.

GOSHAWK

THE GOSHAWK IS THE LARGEST OF THE ACIPITER HAWKS. THEY ARE FOREST DWELLING BIRDS WITH SHORT, ROUND WINGS AND LONG TAILS. THE GOSHAWK'S DIET CON- SISTS MAINLY OF OTHER BIRDS WHICH ARE OFTEN TAKEN IN FLIGHT. CONSEQUENTLY, THE GOSHAWK IS EXTREMELY FAST AND CAPABLE OF SPECTACULAR AERIAL MANOEUVERING. IF THE OP- PORTUNITY ARISES IT WILL CON- DUCT A LIGHTNING-LIKE RAID ON FARMYARD FOWL, WITH VARIOUS OTHER HAWKS GETTING THE BLAME.

THE ADULT GOSHAWK IS BLUE- GREY WITH A DARKER HEAD AND NEAR WHITE UNDERPARTS. THE YOUNGER GOSHAWK IS DARK BROWN WITH A CREAMY UNDERSIDE WELL STREAKED WITH BROWN. THE FULLY GROWN BIRD HAS A WINGSPREAD OF ABOUT 120 CM (48 IN.).

ADULT

JUVENILE

THE NEST IS CONSTRUCTED OF TWIGS, STICKS, AND LEAVES AND IS USUALLY FOUND HIGH IN AN EVERGREEN DEEP IN THE MOUNTAIN FOREST.

THE GOSHAWK TAKES A CONSIDERABLE TOLL OF WESTERN CANADA'S GROUSE, PARTRIDGE, AND PHEASANT, AS WELL AS MANY OF OUR SMALLER BIRDS, ALTHOUGH IT IS ONLY PLAYING THE ROLE WHICH NATURE INTENDED.

RED-TAILED HAWK

DURING SUMMER THE RED-TAILED HAWK IN-HABITS ALMOST ALL OF CANADA, AND IS OFTEN SEEN CIRCLING SLOWLY AT HIGH ALTITUDES. THE RED-TAILED IS A LARGE HAWK MORE THAN 50 CM (19 IN.) LONG. THE ADULT IS IDENTIFIED BY THE BRICK-RED COLOR OF ITS UPPER TAIL SUR-FACE.

THE RED-TAIL'S NEST IS USUALLY HIGH IN A TREE IN FAIRLY OPEN FOREST. THE BULKY NEST IS MADE OF STICKS AND TWIGS, LINED WITH MOSS, LICHEN, AND OTHER SOFT MATERIALS. THE TWO OR THREE EGGS MAY BE WHITE OR SPLOTCHED WITH PALE BROWN.

THE FOOD OF THIS HAWK INCLUDES GROUNDSQUIRRELS, RED SQUIR-RELS, GOPHERS, CHIPMUNKS AND OTHER RODENTS, AS WELL AS SNAKES AND LARGER INSECTS. A FEW DEVELOP A TASTE FOR DOMESTIC FOWL AND GIVE ALL SPECIES A BAD NAME. OVERALL, HOWEVER, THE RED-TAILED HAWK IS BENEFICIAL TO FARMERS. FOR THIS REASON MOST PROVINCES HAVE LAWS PROHIBITING THE DESTRUCTION OF THEM OR THEIR EGGS.

 GOLDEN EAGLE

THE GOLDEN EAGLE IS MAGNIFICENTLY AT-
TUNED TO THE AIR. IT USES UPDRAFTS TO
CARRY IT TO LOFTY HEIGHTS WHERE IT
BECOMES A SPECK IN THE BLUE AND IS
CREDITED WITH BEING
ABLE TO DIVE AT
100 KPH (60 MPH.).

THIS LARGE BIRD OF PREY
DINES ON MARMOTS,
RABBITS, LARGE RODENTS,
WATERFOWL, AND, ON
OCCASION, FOXES. IT ALSO
FEEDS ON THE CARCASSES
OF MOUNTAIN SHEEP, DEER,
AND OTHER ANIMALS.

ADULT
GOLDEN EAGLE

ADULT
BALD EAGLE

THE GOLDEN EAGLE RANGES THROUGH-
OUT THE NORTHERN HEMISPHERE,
USUALLY IN REMOTE MOUNTAIN
AREAS. EACH BIRD CLAIMS A LARGE
TERRITORY FOR EXCLUSIVE HUNTING
AND QUICKLY DRIVES OFF INTRUDERS.
CONTRARY TO NATURE'S GENERAL
RULE, THE FEMALE IS THE LARGER OF
THE SPECIES AND CAN HAVE A
WINGSPREAD OF MORE THAN 2M
(7 FT.).

ITS NEST IS SITUATED ON A ROCKY
LEDGE OR ON TOP OF A TALL SNAG
OVERLOOKING A VAST AREA. BOTH
PARENTS INCUBATE THE EGGS,
USUALLY TWO IN NUMBER, WHICH
HATCH IN APPROXIMATELY SIX WEEKS.

THE GOLDEN EAGLE'S REAR TALONS
ARE MUCH LARGER THAN THOSE
OF THE BALD EAGLE.

BALD EAGLE

IMMATURE

THE BALD EAGLE HAS ONLY TWO NATURAL ENEMIES--
MAN AND THE GREAT HORNED OWL. THE LATTER
HAS BEEN KNOWN TO ROUT THE EAGLE
FROM ITS NEST.

ADULT

THE EAGLE'S LIKING FOR FISH
ACCOUNTS FOR THE MAJORITY
OF THESE GREAT BIRDS NESTING
NEAR THE SEA OR LARGE LAKES.
POWERFUL EYES ENABLE IT TO
SPOT PREY AS FAR AWAY AS
3.2 KM (2 MI.). ITS RAZOR-
SHARP TALONS ARE USED IN
STRIKING AND CARRYING OFF
ITS PREY, WHILE ITS HOOKED
BEAK ENABLES IT TO EASILY
TEAR FLESH. DESPITE THIS
FORMIDABLE EQUIPMENT, THE
EAGLE IS ONLY AN AVERAGE
FISH CATCHER AND OFTEN
ROBS THE OSPREY OF ITS
MEAL.

THE NEST IS USUALLY BUILT AT THE
TOP OF AN OLD TREE OR ON A SHELF
HIGH ON A CLIFF. THE SAME NEST
IS USED YEAR AFTER YEAR BY
THE SAME PAIR OF BIRDS AND RARE-
LY HOLDS MORE THAN TWO WHITE
EGGS.

FOR THE FIRST THREE YEARS OF ITS LIFE THE YOUNG EAGLE
HAS PLUMAGE A GREAT DEAL DARKER THAN THE ADULT BUT
LACKS THE WHITE HEAD AND TAIL. THIS COLORATION IS
RESPONSIBLE FOR MANY FAULTY IDENTIFICATIONS.

MIGRATION PLAYS NO PART IN AN EAGLE'S LIFE. IT LEAVES
ITS TERRITORY ONLY WHEN THE WATER IS FROZEN. LIKE
MANY OTHER SPECIES
OF WILDLIFE, THE
EAGLE POPULATION
IS SLOWLY DE-
CLINING.

OSPREY

THE OSPREY, OR FISH HAWK, GLIDES OVER THE WATER IN SEARCH OF FISH FEEDING NEAR THE SURFACE. WHEN PREY IS SIGHTED, THE LARGE BIRD PLUNGES FEET FIRST INTO THE WATER TO SNATCH ITS VICTIM. IT THEN RISES SWIFTLY AND LIGHTS ON SOME LOFTY PERCH TO DEVOUR ITS CATCH. MALE AND FEMALE ARE SIMILAR IN COLOR; THE FEMALE, HOWEVER, IS SLIGHTLY LARGER THAN HER COUNTERPART.

THE OSPREY'S NEST IS USUALLY BUILT IN A TALL TREE OR, IN AREAS WHERE SUCH TREES ARE NOT FOUND, ON A LEDGE HIGH ON A CLIFF. BOTH MALE AND FEMALE TAKE PART IN THE CON- STRUCTION OF THE NEST. THE SAME NEST MAY BE USED YEAR AFTER YEAR BUT BECAUSE IT IS REPAIRED AN- NUALLY AND OFTEN ENLARGED, IT CAN BECOME ALMOST 2M (6 FT.) ACROSS AND 1.5 M (5 FT.) DEEP.

THE FEMALE LAYS TWO OR THREE EGGS AND AFTER THE YOUNG HATCH SHE DOES MOST OF THE REARING. THE MALE CARRIES ON WITH HIS FISHING AND BRINGS FOOD TO HIS MATE AND YOUNG. THE LITTLE OSPREYS MAY REMAIN IN THE NEST FOR ALMOST TWO MONTHS.

AN EAGLE OFTEN WAITS FOR AN OSPREY TO CATCH A FISH AND, WHILE THE THE OSPREY IS IN THE AIR, ATTACKS AND CAUSES IT TO DROP THE FISH WHICH THE EAGLE QUICKLY RETRIEVES.

UNLIKE OTHER HAWKS, THE OSPREY'S OUTER TOE IS REVERSIBLE. THIS ADAPTATION, COUPLED WITH THE ROUGHLY SCALED PADS ON THE BOTTOM OF ITS TOES, ENABLE IT TO GRASP A SLIP- PERY FISH IN SUCH A MANNER THAT IT CANNOT POSSIBLY ESCAPE.

PEREGRINE FALCON

ALTHOUGH IT IS COMPARATIVELY RARE, THE PEREGRINE FALCON, OR DUCK HAWK AS IT IS COMMONLY KNOWN, INHABITS MANY AREAS OF CANADA. IT IS OFTEN CONFUSED WITH THE PRAIRIE FALCON WHICH IS SIMILAR IN APPEARANCE. THE FEMALE PEREGRINE LOOKS MUCH LIKE THE MALE BUT IS A LITTLE LARGER AND MAY GROW TO 51 CM (20 IN.).

THE PEREGRINE'S NEST IS USUALLY IN A CRANNY HIGH ON AN INACCESSIBLE CLIFF, BUT SOME-TIMES IN NATURAL CAVITIES IN TREES. THE THREE OR FOUR DULL WHITE EGGS ARE LIBERALLY SPLOTCHED WITH BROWN AND RED. THE PEREGRINE HAS FEW ENEMIES, THE WORST BEING COLLECTORS OF BIRDS' EGGS AND THE FORMER WIDESPREAD USE OF THE INSECT-ICIDE DDT.

THIS FALCON'S USUAL METHOD OF CAP-TURING PREY IS TO RISE IN SPIRALS THEN PLUMMET DOWN, ALTHOUGH A SUDDEN ASSAULT OR DIRECT CHASE MAY BE USED. TO ITS DISCREDIT, THE PEREGRINE SOMETIMES STRIKES BIRD AFTER BIRD IN A FLOCK, LEAV-ING THEM WHERE THEY FALL. ON BALANCE, HOWEVER, IT IS BENEFIC-IAL TO MAN.

SPARROW HAWK

THE SPARROW HAWK, THE SMALLEST MEMBER OF THE FALCON FAMILY, IS ALSO KNOWN AS THE AMERICAN KESTREL. NO LARGER THAN A ROBIN BUT EVERY INCH A HAWK, THIS LITTLE FALCON MAY BE FOUND THROUGHOUT WESTERN CANADA, USUALLY IN OPEN AREAS AND AROUND PASTURES.

ITS DIET CONSISTS OF RODENTS, SMALL BIRDS, AND INSECTS. FOR THIS REASON LARGE NUMBERS OF THEM ARE OFTEN SEEN IN AREAS INFESTED WITH GRASSHOPPERS. IT IS ALSO A VALUABLE ALLY IN MAN'S ON-GOING BATTLE TO CONTROL RODENT POPULATIONS.

THE SPARROW HAWK'S NEST IS USUALLY BUILT IN HOLES IN CLIFFS OR TREES. THE NEST CONTAINS FOUR OR FIVE SMALL WHITE EGGS WITH BROWN SPECKS.

SHARP-TAILED GROUSE

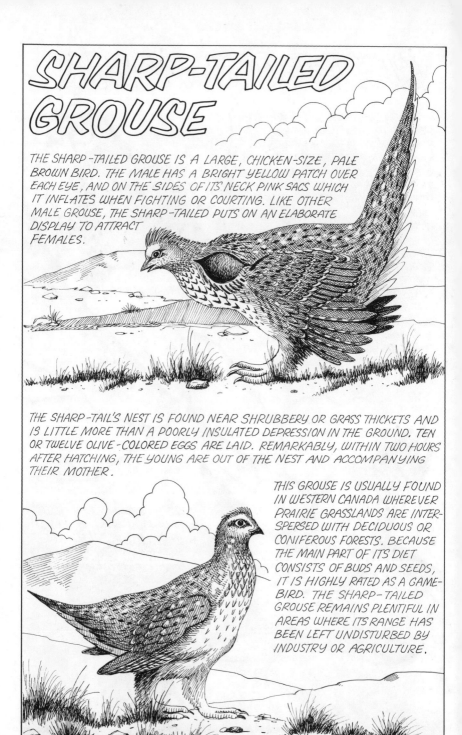

THE SHARP-TAILED GROUSE IS A LARGE, CHICKEN-SIZE, PALE BROWN BIRD. THE MALE HAS A BRIGHT YELLOW PATCH OVER EACH EYE, AND ON THE SIDES OF ITS NECK PINK SACS WHICH IT INFLATES WHEN FIGHTING OR COURTING. LIKE OTHER MALE GROUSE, THE SHARP-TAILED PUTS ON AN ELABORATE DISPLAY TO ATTRACT FEMALES.

THE SHARP-TAIL'S NEST IS FOUND NEAR SHRUBBERY OR GRASS THICKETS AND IS LITTLE MORE THAN A POORLY INSULATED DEPRESSION IN THE GROUND. TEN OR TWELVE OLIVE-COLORED EGGS ARE LAID. REMARKABLY, WITHIN TWO HOURS AFTER HATCHING, THE YOUNG ARE OUT OF THE NEST AND ACCOMPANYING THEIR MOTHER.

THIS GROUSE IS USUALLY FOUND IN WESTERN CANADA WHEREVER PRAIRIE GRASSLANDS ARE INTERSPERSED WITH DECIDUOUS OR CONIFEROUS FORESTS. BECAUSE THE MAIN PART OF ITS DIET CONSISTS OF BUDS AND SEEDS, IT IS HIGHLY RATED AS A GAME-BIRD. THE SHARP-TAILED GROUSE REMAINS PLENTIFUL IN AREAS WHERE ITS RANGE HAS BEEN LEFT UNDISTURBED BY INDUSTRY OR AGRICULTURE.

RUFFED GROUSE

THE RUFFED GROUSE INHABITS ALMOST ALL OF CANADA, INCLUDING CONIFER FORESTS, BUSHLANDS, AND OPEN FIELDS.

IT CAN BE REDDISH OR GREYISH, WITH BIRDS OF BOTH COLOR VARIATIONS OCCUPYING THE SAME AREA. IT USUALLY WEIGHS JUST OVER .5 KG (1 LB.), IS ABOUT 43 CM (17 IN.) LONG, AND FLIES UP TO 35 KPH (22 MPH).

IN THE SPRING A FAMILIAR SOUND TO WOODS TRAVELLERS IS THE MALE GROUSE DRUMMING -- THE MALE RAPIDLY FLAPPING ITS WINGS. AT THE SAME TIME IT DISPLAYS ITS TAIL IN A FAN SHAPE, BOTH ACTIONS DESIGNED TO ATTRACT THE FEMALE. THE MALE MATES WITH SEVERAL HENS WHICH LAY NINE TO TWELVE BUFF-COLORED EGGS IN NESTS ON THE GROUND.

THE RUFFED GROUSE POPULATION FLUCTUATES WIDELY. YEARS OF HIGH POPULATION ARE FOLLOWED BY THOSE OF EXTREMELY LOW IN A CYCLE THAT OCCURS ABOUT EVERY TEN YEARS. CHIEF ENEMIES OF THE GROUSE ARE HAWKS, OWLS, AND MAN.

PTARMIGAN

THERE ARE THREE SPECIES OF PTARMIGAN IN CANADA -- THE WHITE-TAILED, TOP, THE ROCK, CENTER, AND THE WILLOW, BOTTOM. ALL ARE FOUND IN THE NORTHERN PART OF WESTERN CANADA.

THE BIRDS SHOWN ARE ALL MALES. THE FEMALES OF THE THREE SPECIES ARE LESS IMPRESSIVE AND SIMILAR TO EACH OTHER IN APPEARANCE AND HABITS. THE PTARMIGAN PREFERS COLDER CLIMES AND HIGH ALTITUDES. ITS LEGS AND FEET ARE FEATHERED FOR WARMTH AND IN WINTER ITS PLUMAGE TURNS WHITE. WHATEVER THE SEASON, IT IS WELL CAMOUFLAGED AND WHEN SITTING ON THE GROUND IS ALMOST IMPOSSIBLE TO SEE.

THE PTARMIGAN FEEDS MAINLY ON ALPINE BERRIES, SEEDS, AND INSECTS, EXCEPT IN WINTER WHEN SNOW DRIVES IT BELOW TIMBERLINE. HERE IT FEEDS ON TWIGS AND BUDS OF ALDER AND WILLOW.

ITS NEST IS BUILT ON THE GROUND, USUALLY IN THE SHELTER OF A ROCK OR HUMMOCK. IT IS LINED WITH MOSS, GRASS, AND FEATHERS AND CONTAINS SIX TO EIGHT EGGS.

QUAIL

THE QUAIL SEEN HERE WERE ALL INTRODUCED INTO BRITISH CO-LUMBIA. ONLY THE CALIFORNIA QUAIL, LEFT, HAS SUCCESS-FULLY SURVIVED. IT WAS INTRODUCED INTO B.C. IN THE NINETEENTH CENTURY AND HAS DONE WELL IN THE SOUTHERN INTERIOR AND FAIRLY WELL ON VANCOUVER ISLAND. THIS SMALL PLUMP QUAIL, ABOUT 25 CM (10 IN.) LONG, IS EASILY RECOGNIZED BY THE SMALL PLUME ON TOP OF ITS HEAD. THE MALE STANDS GUARD WHILE THE FEMALE INCUBATES AS MANY AS TWENTY EGGS. LIKE OTHER QUAIL, ITS FOOD CONSISTS MAINLY OF GRASS, SEEDS, AND FRUIT, AS WELL AS DOMESTIC GRAINS WHEN AVAILABLE.

THE MOUNTAIN QUAIL, RIGHT, WAS INTRODUCED INTO B.C. IN THE LAST HALF OF THE NINETEENTH CENTURY. IT IS NOW SEEN ONLY RARELY IN THE SOUTHERN PORTION OF VANCOUVER ISLAND. THIS BIRD, A LITTLE LARGER THAN THE CAL-IFORNIA QUAIL, CAN ALSO BE IDENTIFIED BY ITS PLUME WHICH IS LONGER, STRAIGHTER, AND THINNER THAN THAT OF THE CALIFORNIA QUAIL.

THE BOB-WHITE QUAIL, LEFT, IS A LITTLE SMALLER THAN THE CAL-IFORNIA QUAIL BUT IS A VERY POPULAR AND EDIBLE GAME BIRD IN THE UNITED STATES. IT WAS INTRODUCED INTO B.C. IN THE TWENTIETH CENTURY, SURVIVED INITIALLY, BUT DISAPPEARED AFTER A FEW YEARS.

RINGNECK PHEASANT

THE RINGNECK, OR CHINESE, PHEASANT WAS FIRST INTRODUCED INTO WESTERN CANADA IN THE 1890S. TODAY IT IS FOUND ALMOST ANYWHERE THERE IS SUITABLE HABITAT.

THE RINGNECK IS ACTUALLY A PRODUCT OF INTERBREEDING THREE SPECIES OF ORIENTAL PHEASANTS. THE COCK PHEASANT MAY MEASURE ALMOST 1M (3 FT.) INCLUDING ITS BEAUTIFUL TAIL. THE RINGNECK'S SPECTACULAR COLORING RANGES FROM THE METALLIC GREEN OF ITS HEAD TO THE MANY SHADES OF COPPER AND GOLD ON ITS SIDES AND BACK.

THE RINGNECK IS A FAVORITE OF UPLAND GAME HUNTERS BECAUSE OF ITS SIZE, BEAUTY, AND SWIFTNESS OF FLIGHT. SINCE ITS FLESH IS EXCELLENT, IT RETAINS THE TITLE "KING OF THE GAMEBIRDS" EVEN WHEN ON A PLATTER.

IN SPRING THE COCK PHEASANT STAKES OUT ITS TERRITORY AND DEFENDS IT VISCIOUSLY. HE COLLECTS A HAREM OF HENS THAT BUILD NESTS IN HOLLOWS IN THE GROUND, USUALLY WITH ADEQUATE BRUSH FOR COVER. THE HENS LAY UP TO FIFTEEN GREY-GREEN EGGS WHICH HATCH AFTER AN INCUBATION PERIOD OF TWENTY-TWO DAYS. THE YOUNG GROW QUICKLY AND ARE USUALLY ABLE TO FLY WITHIN THREE WEEKS.

PHEASANTS FEED CHIEFLY ON WEED SEEDS, GRAIN, WILD FRUIT, AND INSECTS. TO THE ANNOYANCE OF FARMERS, HOWEVER, MANY LIKE TO ASSIST IN THE HARVESTING OF CROPS SUCH AS POTATOES AND STRAWBERRIES.

KILLDEER

THE KILLDEER, OR KILLDEER PLOVER, IS COMMON THROUGH-OUT MOST OF CANADA WHER-EVER THERE ARE BEACHES, MUD FLATS, FARMS OR OPEN COUNTRY. THE KILLDEER'S NEST IS NOTHING MORE THAN A SHALLOW DEPRESSION LINED WITH STONES AND PEBBLES. THE EGGS, USUALLY FOUR, HATCH AFTER FOUR WEEKS OF INCUBATION BY BOTH MALE AND FEMALE PARENTS. IN ONLY A FEW HOURS CHICKS ARE RUNNING ABOUT ON STRONG LEGS, FORAGING FOR FOOD WITH THEIR PARENTS. THE YOUNG HAVE ONLY ONE DARK BAND ON THEIR NECKS WHILE ADULTS HAVE TWO.

BECAUSE OF THE EXPOSED POSITION OF THE KILLDEER'S NEST, THE BIRD IS AN EXPERT AT USING THE "BROKEN WING TRICK." INTRUDERS ARE DRAWN AWAY FROM THE NEST BY THE PAR-ENT BIRD STUMBLING ALONG WITH ONE WING DRAGGING ON THE GROUND. WHEN THE INTRUDER HAS BEEN LURED FAR ENOUGH, THE KILLDEER SUD-DENLY RECOVERS AND FLIES AWAY.

CURLEW

THE CURLEW IS A LARGE BUFF-COLORED BIRD SEEN IN WESTERN CANADA IN THE SPRING AND FALL. IT NESTS IN THE ARCTIC TUNDRA AND WINTERS ON THE WEST COAST OF SOUTH AMERICA. DURING MIGRATION IT FLIES WITH OTHER CURLEWS IN LONG V FORMATIONS AND AT NIGHT ROOSTS AND SETTLES ON MARSHY ISLANDS OR SAND BARS.

THE CURLEW, WHICH STANDS ABOUT 30 CM (12 IN.) HIGH ON LONG, THIN LEGS, IS A WIDE-RANGING BIRD AND IN OTHER COUNTRIES IS KNOWN AS THE WHIMBREL. IT LIVES IN PLACES AS DIVERSE AS SCOTLAND AND EURASIA, AFRICA, RUSSIA, AND THE SOUTH PACIFIC. BUT REGARDLESS OF WHERE IT LIVES, IT IS ALWAYS FOUND IN COASTAL AREAS AND NEAR FRESH WATER.

CHIEF IDENTIFYING MARKS ARE A STRIPED HEAD AND LENGTHY DOWN-CURVED BILL, IDEAL FOR POKING IN MUD-FLATS FOR WORMS, CRUSTACEANS AND ASSORTED INSECTS. FOUR GREY-GREEN EGGS SPOTTED WITH BROWN ARE LAID IN A NEST THAT IS CONSTRUCTED ON THE GROUND.

THE CURLEW THAT INHABITS CANADA'S PACIFIC COAST IS THE HUDSONIAN. WHILE OTHER SPECIES ARE UNFORTUNATELY APPROACHING EXTINCTION, THE HUDSONIAN APPEARS TO BE INCREASING.

GULLS

THE CALIFORNIA GULL, LEFT, IS USUALLY JUST A MIGRANT IN B.C., GENERALLY SEEN IN AUGUST OR SEPTEMBER. IT NESTS ON THE GROUND IN LARGE COLONIES NEAR PRAIRIE LAKES.

THE BLACK HEAD OF THE BONA-PARTE GULL, A CLOSE RELATIVE OF THE FRANKLIN GULL, FACIL-ITATES INSTANT RECOGNITION. THIS GULL CAN BE SEEN IN THE PRAIRIE PROVINCES AS WELL AS IN B.C. UNLIKE OTHER GULLS, THE BONAPARTE IS A TREE NEST-ER, USUALLY IN CONIFERS CLOSE TO WATER.

HEERMANN'S GULL, BELOW, IS EASILY RECOGNIZED BY ITS DIRTY-BROWN BACK AND WING-TOPS, AND ITS RED BEAK. THIS GULL IS SEEN MOST OFTEN AROUND B.C.'S GULF ISLANDS WHERE IT FEEDS MAINLY ON HERRING.

A PERMANENT RESIDENT OF BRITISH COLUMBIA'S COAST-LINE, THE GLAUCOUS-WINGED GULL, IS FREQUENTLY FOUND SCAVENGING ON CITY DUMPS. IT IS ONE OF THE LARGER GULLS, OFTEN REACHING 68CM (27 IN.). WHEN FOOD IS SCARCE, THIS GULL HAS BEEN KNOWN TO KILL AND DEVOUR YOUNG, SICK, OR CRIPPLED DUCKS. ON THE BRIGHTER SIDE, THE GLAUCOUS-WINGED GULL IS OUR NUMBER ONE BEACH CLEANER AND, LIKE ALL GULLS, IS PROTECTED BY LAW.

77

ARCTIC TERN

THE ARCTIC TERN MAKES ONE OF THE LONGEST MIGRATORY FLIGHTS OF ANY BIRD IN THE WORLD, SOME 18,000 KM (11,000 MI.) FROM ITS ARCTIC NESTING GROUND TO ITS ANTARCTIC WINTERING GROUND. WHILE THE MAJORITY OF THESE BIRDS IN THEIR MIGRATORY FLIGHT TRAVEL PARALLEL TO BRITISH COLUMBIA'S COAST BUT FAR OUT TO SEA, THEY HAVE ALSO BEEN SEEN TRAVELING THROUGH THE INTERIOR OF THE PROVINCE.

THE EGGS ARE LAID IN A NEST ON THE GROUND AND BY LATE AUGUST THE CHICKS ARE ABLE TO JOIN THEIR PARENTS IN THEIR INCREDIBLY LONG FLIGHT SOUTH.

THE ARCTIC TERN IS ABOUT THE SIZE OF A PIGEON. IN COLOR IT IS BASICALLY WHITE AND GREY WITH A BLACK CAP AND WING TIPS. ITS DEEPLY FORKED TAIL DISTINGUISHES IT FROM THE COMMON TERN.

MOURNING DOVE

THE MOURNING DOVE, WHILE RARE ON THE PACIFIC COAST EXCEPT DURING MIGRATION, IS FAIRLY ABUNDANT IN MANY AREAS OF SOUTHERN CANADA. THIS BIRD IS USUALLY FOUND IN OPEN COUNTRY THAT IS LIBERALLY LACED WITH THICKETS AND GROVES OF DECIDUOUS TREES. IT IS USUALLY SEEN EITHER SINGLY OR IN PAIRS, SELDOM IN GROUPS. IT HAS, PARTICULARLY IN PAST YEARS, BEEN MISTAKEN FOR THE EXTINCT PASSENGER PIGEON.

THE MALE MOURNING DOVE HAS A LONG TAIL WITH SHORT, WHITE AND BLACK OUTER FEATHERS. ITS UNDERSIDE IS A SOFT WARM BUFF COLOR, WHILE ITS BACK IS BLUISH-GREY. THE FEMALE LOOKS MUCH LIKE THE MALE BUT IS SMALLER, LESS COLORFUL, AND HAS A SHORTER TAIL. THE DOVE'S WALK IS SIMILAR TO THAT OF A PIGEON-- SHORT QUICK STEPS AND A BOBBING HEAD.

THE MOURNING DOVE IS A POOR NEST BUILDER. ITS NEST IS USUALLY QUITE FLIMSY AND BARELY ADEQUATE TO HOLD THE USUAL TWO EGGS. WHEN TREES ARE NOT AVAILABLE, THE MOURNING DOVE READILY NESTS UPON THE GROUND. BOTH PARENTS TAKE TURNS SITTING ON THE EGGS WHICH HATCH IN TWELVE TO FOURTEEN DAYS. THE YOUNG FEED ON PRE-DIGESTED FOOD FROM THEIR PARENTS' CROPS. WHILE THE MOURNING DOVE USUALLY SETS ONLY TWO EGGS AT A TIME, THE POPULATION IS MAINTAINED BY TWO, THREE, OR MORE BROODS A YEAR IN SOUTHERN CLIMES.

THE MOURNING DOVE'S DIET IS BENEFICIAL TO MAN SINCE IT CONSISTS MAINLY OF WEED SEEDS AND INSECTS, PARTICULARLY GRASSHOPPERS.

SCREECH OWL

THE SCREECH OWL OCCURS IN TWO COLOR PHASES--GREY AND RED-BROWN. IT IS SELDOM LONGER THAN 25 CM (10 IN.), THE SMALLEST OF THE OWLS WHICH HAVE EAR TUFTS.

IT DOES SOME TRAVELING BUT IS NOT KNOWN TO MIGRATE.

THIS LITTLE OWL FREQUENTLY NESTS IN AN ABANDONED WOODPECKER'S HOLE. FOUR OR FIVE WHITE EGGS, ROUND, RATHER THAN EGG SHAPED, ARE LAID IN A NEST WHICH IS OFTEN SHARED BY BOTH PARENTS DURING THE DAY. THE EGGS HATCH AFTER TWENTY-FOUR DAYS, WITH THE YOUNG OWL BLIND FOR THE FIRST TWO WEEKS. IT HAS PURE WHITE PLUMAGE, AND IS SEVERAL MONTHS OLD BEFORE IT RESEMBLES ITS PARENTS.

THE SCREECH OWL DINES LARGE-LY ON MICE, FROGS, AND SNAKES. GRASSHOPPERS, MOTHS, AND OTHER INSECTS ARE ALSO EATEN WHEN AVAILABLE. IT, IN TURN, IS PREYED UPON BY LARGER OWLS. DESPITE ITS SMALL SIZE, THE SCREECH OWL IS CONSIDERED BENEFICIAL TO FARMERS AND ORCHARDISTS.

SNOWY OWL

THE SNOWY OWL IS A LARGE BIRD. A LENGTH OF 62CM (24 IN.) IS NOT UNCOMMON. DEPENDING ON THE SEASON, THIS MAGNIFICENT OWL CAN BE SEEN FROM THE ARCTIC TUNDRA TO CANADA'S SOUTHERN BORDER. ALTHOUGH ITS HOME IS THE ARCTIC, IN WINTER A SHORTAGE OF FOOD OFTEN DRIVES IT SOUTHWARD. HOW FAR SOUTH IT MIGRATES DEPENDS ENTIRELY ON THE SEVERITY OF THE WINTER AND ABUNDANCE OF FOOD. BUT SINCE THE SNOWY HAS NO HOMING INSTINCT, FEW, IF ANY, EVER RETURN TO THE ARCTIC.

ON THE ARCTIC BREEDING GROUND ITS NEST, LINED WITH DRY GRASS, IS FOUND IN A DEPRESSION ON THE GROUND, AND GENERALLY CONTAINS FIVE TO SEVEN WHITE OR CREAM-COLORED EGGS.

BECAUSE OF THE LONG SUMMER DAYS IN THE NORTH, THE SNOWY MUST HUNT IN DAYLIGHT. WHILE IT IS A VORACIOUS CONSUMER OF RODENTS, IT DOES ON OCCASION KILL PTARMIGANS, DUCKS, AND ARCTIC HARES, WHICH ARE OFTEN TWICE ITS OWN WEIGHT. THERE HAVE BEEN REPORTS THAT THE SNOWY OWL IS ALSO AN EXPERT AT CATCHING FISH.

KINGFISHER

A NOISY, ENERGETIC BIRD, THE BELTED KINGFISHER IS OFTEN SEEN PERCHED ON A BRANCH ABOVE THE WATER PATIENTLY WAITING FOR DINNER TO SWIM INTO VIEW. AT THE APPROPRIATE MOMENT IT MAKES A MISSILE-LIKE DIVE, HITTING THE WATER WITH A RESOUNDING SPLASH AND SOON EMERGES, PREY HELD TIGHTLY IN ITS BILL. ON REGAINING ITS PERCH IT QUICKLY SWALLOWS THE FISH HEADFIRST.

THE KINGFISHER IS EASILY IDENTIFIED BY ITS LARGE BEAK AND HEAD TOPPED BY AN UNRULY CREST. THE MALE IS GREY-BLUE AND WHITE. UNLIKE MOST BIRDS, HOWEVER, THE FEMALE IS THE MOST COLORFUL AND HAS A RUST-COLORED BAR ACROSS HER BREAST.

THE KINGFISHER, OFTEN FOUND IN PAIRS THROUGHOUT THE YEAR, IS A SOMEWHAT QUARRELSOME BIRD. ITS EAR-SPLITTING CRY CARRIES FOR SOME DISTANCE, WARNING OTHERS OF THE SPECIES TO STAY IN THEIR OWN AREA.

AT NESTING TIME THIS BUSY BIRD TUNNELS ABOUT 1 M (3 FT.) INTO A BANK TO LAY SIX TO TEN WHITE EGGS IN A SMALL CHAMBER. BOTH MALE AND FEMALE INCUBATE THE EGGS.

IT IS A FRIEND TO THE SPORTSMAN SINCE IT EATS MANY CHUB AND OTHER FISH THAT ARE HARMFUL TO YOUNG TROUT.

STELLER JAY

THE STELLER JAY, A MEM-
BER OF THE CROW FAMILY,
RESEMBLES THE BLUE JAY OF
EASTERN CANADA IN SIZE
AND SHAPE, BUT ONLY ITS
TAIL, WING EXTREMITIES,
AND A SMALL PATCH OVER
EACH EYE ARE BLUE. THE
REMAINDER OF THE BIRD IS
BLACK. BOLD AND INQUISI-
TIVE, THE STELLER JAY IS
COMMON AROUND CAMP-
SITES WHERE IT SEARCHES
FOR HANDOUTS. ITS NORMAL
FOOD, HOWEVER, CONSISTS
OF GRAIN, NUTS, BERRIES,
FRUIT, INSECTS, AND CARRION.

LIKE ALL BIRDS OF THE
CROW FAMILY, THIS JAY
IS ABLE TO ADAPT EASILY
TO MOST SITUATIONS. IT
IS FOUND FROM SEA LEVEL
TO HIGH IN THE MOUN-
TAINS AND EVEN IN THE
SUBURBS OF CITIES. IT
BUILDS AN AWKWARD
NEST OF TWIGS AND MUD,
USUALLY IN A FIR TREE.
IN EARLY SPRING FOUR OR
FIVE PALE GREEN EGGS ARE
LAID AND TWO MONTHS
LATER THE YOUNG ARE
ALREADY OUT FORAGING.

MAGPIE

NO OTHER BIRD RESEMBLES THE MAGPIE. THIS LARGE BLACK AND WHITE SPECIES WITH ITS LONG TAIL IS A YEAR-ROUND RESIDENT OF WESTERN CANADA EXCEPT IN THE PACIFIC COAST AREA. OPEN LAND WITH READILY AVAILABLE COVER IS ITS PREFERRED HABITAT. LIKE ITS CLOSE RELATIVE, THE CROW, THE MAGPIE IS CLEVER AND NOT EASY TO APPROACH.

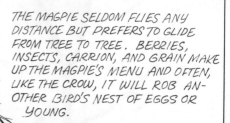

THE MAGPIE SELDOM FLIES ANY DISTANCE BUT PREFERS TO GLIDE FROM TREE TO TREE. BERRIES, INSECTS, CARRION, AND GRAIN MAKE UP THE MAGPIE'S MENU AND OFTEN, LIKE THE CROW, IT WILL ROB ANOTHER BIRD'S NEST OF EGGS OR YOUNG.

YOUNG MAGPIES

THE MAGPIE'S NEST IS A BULKY STRUCTURE OF ROOTS AND TWIGS. IT USUALLY HAS A ROOF AND AN ENTRANCE HOLE IN THE SIDE. FIVE TO TEN EGGS ARE LAID IN APRIL. THE MAGPIE FLEDGLING HAS A STUBBY LITTLE TAIL QUITE UNLIKE THAT OF THE ADULT.

CROW

TWO SPECIES OF CROWS INHABIT WESTERN CANADA. ON B.C.'S COAST IS THE NORTHWESTERN CROW, WHILE ON THE PRAIRIES IS THE COMMON, OR AMERICAN, CROW. THE TWO BIRDS ARE SIMILAR IN APPEARANCE, THE ONLY DIFFERENCE IS THAT THE PRAIRIE CROW IS CONSIDERABLY LARGER.

THE CROW IS NOT A FUSSY EATER, IN FACT IT EATS ANYTHING AVAILABLE -- FRUIT, CARRION, FROGS, SEASHORE LIFE, YOUNG BIRDS AND EGGS WHICH THE CROW IS PARTICULARLY ADEPT AT STEALING FROM NESTS. IT IS ALSO MISCHIEVOUS AND SLY. IT EASILY MIMICS OTHER BIRDS AND ANIMALS AND MAY EVEN BE TAUGHT TO SAY A FEW WORDS.

THE CROW'S NEST IS GENERALLY HIGH IN A TREE, WITH SMALL GROUPS USUALLY NESTING TOGETHER. THE NEST IS CONSTRUCTED OF COARSE MATERIALS SUCH AS STICKS, TWIGS, AND BARK, AND MAY BE LINED WITH MOSS, WOOL OR ROTTED WOOD. DURING NEST BUILDING THE CROW IS NOT AVERSE TO STEALING CHOICE BITS OF MATERIAL FROM A NEIGHBOR'S NEST. USUALLY, THERE ARE FOUR OR FIVE OLIVE-COLORED EGGS SPLOTCHED WITH BROWN.

THE CROW IS REMARKABLY ADAPTABLE AND IN SPITE OF MAN'S RELENTLESS WAR ON IT, CONTINUES TO THRIVE.

CHICKADEES

FOUR SPECIES OF THE CHICKADEE ARE FOUND IN WESTERN CANADA. THEY ARE USUALLY SEEN IN FLOCKS BUSILY SEARCHING TREES FOR INSECTS.

THE CHESTNUT-BACKED CHICKADEE IS EASILY IDENTIFIED BY ITS REDDISH-BROWN BACK. THE ADULT BIRD, IN SPITE OF ITS SMALL SIZE, BRAVELY WILL DEFEND ITS NEST AGAINST THE ATTACKS OF MUCH LARGER ENEMIES.

THE DISTINCT BLACK CAP AND BIB ARE IDENTIFYING MARKS OF THE BLACK-CAPPED CHICKADEE. ALL FOUR CHICKADEE SPECIES ARE SIMILAR IN SIZE AND SHAPE, NONE LARGER THAN 15 CM (6 IN.) FROM BILL TO TAIL. BECAUSE THEY ARE ABLE TO SURVIVE IN ADVERSE WEATHER, THEY ARE YEAR-ROUND RESIDENTS.

A GENERALLY BROWN COLORING RATHER THAN BLACK AND GREY IDENTIFIES THE BOREAL CHICKADEE. IN THE SPRING ALL CHICKADEE FLOCKS BREAK UP AS PAIRS FLY OFF TO BEGIN THE PROCESS OF MATING. A NEST IS EXCAVATED IN A PUNKY TREE WHERE THE FEMALE LAYS FIVE TO TEN TINY EGGS.

THE MOUNTAIN CHICKADEE HAS A WHITE BAR OVER ITS EYE. LIKE OTHER CHICKADEES, IT FEEDS CHIEFLY ON INSECTS, INSECT EGGS, AND LARVAE. SINCE THE MOUNTAIN CHICKADEE DWELLS MAINLY IN CONIFEROUS FORESTS, IT IS BENEFICIAL TO THE FOREST INDUSTRIES, ALTHOUGH ALL SPECIES SERVE MAN WELL.

ROBIN

THE ROBIN IS FOUND ALMOST EVERYWHERE IN CANADA. WHILE MOST MIGRATE TO CALIFORNIA IN WINTER, MANY REMAIN IN THE MILDER AREAS OF SOUTHERN CANADA.

THIS FAMILIAR BIRD EATS BERRIES, SEEDS, WORMS, AND INSECTS, AND OFTEN BECOMES A NUISANCE IN AREAS WHERE STRAWBERRIES OR CHERRIES ARE GROWN. ALTHOUGH MALE AND FEMALE ARE SIMILAR IN COLOR, THE MALE'S BREAST IS A BRIGHTER SHADE OF ORANGE.

ROBINS NEST IN MOST AREAS OF CANADA. FOUR OR FIVE EGGS ARE LAID IN EARLY SPRING AND HATCH AFTER SEVENTEEN DAYS OF INCUBATION. THE ROBIN'S EGG IS SUCH A BEAUTIFUL HUE THAT A SHADE, ROBIN'S EGG BLUE, HAS BEEN NAMED IN ITS HONOR.

SHRIKE

THERE ARE ONLY TWO SPECIES OF THE SHRIKE IN NORTH AMERICA AND BOTH CAN BE FOUND IN WESTERN CANADA. AS ITS NAME SUGGESTS, THE NORTHERN SHRIKE, ABOVE, FREQUENTS THE NORTHERN REGIONS, WHILE THE LOGGERHEAD SHRIKE, AT LEFT, IS SEEN OCCASIONALLY IN SOUTHERN AREAS. IT PREFERS SEMI-OPEN COUNTRY SUCH AS MEADOWS OR MARSHES INTERSPERSED WITH TREES.

THE SHRIKE IS A ROBIN-SIZED BIRD WITH HAWK-LIKE TENDENCIES. HOWEVER, BECAUSE IT DOESN'T HAVE FEET LIKE THOSE OF A HAWK, IT MUST KILL AND CARRY ITS PREY WITH ITS BILL. THE NAME "BUTCHER BIRD" IS OFTEN APPLIED TO THE SHRIKE BECAUSE OF ITS HABIT OF HANGING SMALL BIRDS, RODENTS, INSECTS, AND OTHER FOOD ON THORNS OR IN CROTCHES OF BRANCHES FOR FUTURE USE.

PACIFIC SALMON

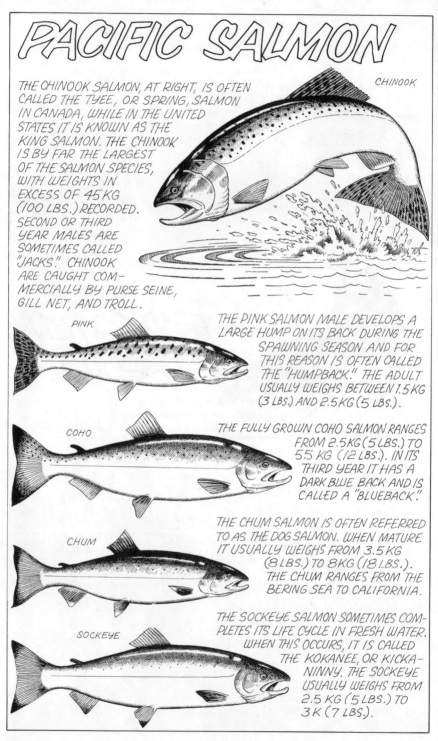

CHINOOK

THE CHINOOK SALMON, AT RIGHT, IS OFTEN CALLED THE TYEE, OR SPRING, SALMON IN CANADA, WHILE IN THE UNITED STATES IT IS KNOWN AS THE KING SALMON. THE CHINOOK IS BY FAR THE LARGEST OF THE SALMON SPECIES, WITH WEIGHTS IN EXCESS OF 45 KG (100 LBS.) RECORDED. SECOND OR THIRD YEAR MALES ARE SOMETIMES CALLED "JACKS." CHINOOK ARE CAUGHT COMMERCIALLY BY PURSE SEINE, GILL NET, AND TROLL.

PINK

THE PINK SALMON MALE DEVELOPS A LARGE HUMP ON ITS BACK DURING THE SPAWNING SEASON AND FOR THIS REASON IS OFTEN CALLED THE "HUMPBACK." THE ADULT USUALLY WEIGHS BETWEEN 1.5 KG (3 LBS.) AND 2.5 KG (5 LBS.).

COHO

THE FULLY GROWN COHO SALMON RANGES FROM 2.5 KG (5 LBS.) TO 5.5 KG (12 LBS.). IN ITS THIRD YEAR IT HAS A DARK BLUE BACK AND IS CALLED A "BLUEBACK."

CHUM

THE CHUM SALMON IS OFTEN REFERRED TO AS THE DOG SALMON. WHEN MATURE IT USUALLY WEIGHS FROM 3.5 KG (8 LBS.) TO 8 KG (18 LBS.). THE CHUM RANGES FROM THE BERING SEA TO CALIFORNIA.

SOCKEYE

THE SOCKEYE SALMON SOMETIMES COMPLETES ITS LIFE CYCLE IN FRESH WATER. WHEN THIS OCCURS, IT IS CALLED THE KOKANEE, OR KICKANINNY. THE SOCKEYE USUALLY WEIGHS FROM 2.5 KG (5 LBS.) TO 3 K (7 LBS.).

THE SOCKEYE CYCLE

THE CYCLE BEGINS IN AUTUMN WHEN THE FEMALE THRESHES A NEST 30 CM (1 FT.) DEEP IN THE GRAVEL OF A RIVER AND DEPOSITS 2 – 3,000 EGGS. THE MALE FERTILIZES THE EGGS BEFORE THE FEMALE COVERS THEM OVER. SEVERAL DAYS LATER BOTH PARENT FISH DIE.

AFTER APPROXIMATELY THIRTY DAYS THE BRIGHT RED EGGS DEVELOP "EYES."

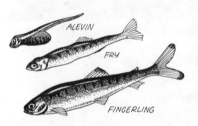

ALEVIN

FRY

FINGERLING

FEBRUARY SEES THE EGGS HATCH AND BECOME ALEVINS, EEL-LIKE CREATURES ATTACHED TO A SAC WHICH CONTAINS A BALANCED DIET AND A METHOD OF EXTRACTING OXYGEN FROM THE WATER. THE ALEVINS REMAIN BENEATH THE GRAVEL FOR THREE OR FOUR MONTHS, GROWING RAPIDLY. A CONTINUAL FLOW OF PURE WATER IS ESSENTIAL TO THEIR SURVIVAL.

THE ALEVINS EMERGE FROM THE GRAVEL MINUS THEIR SACS DURING MAY AND JUNE AND ARE THEN CALLED FRY. THE FRY, 2.5 CM (1 IN.) LONG, MOVE DOWNSTREAM TO A LARGE LAKE WHERE THEY STAY FOR A YEAR BEFORE BE- COMING FINGERLINGS. IN MAY THE FINGERLINGS, NOW ABOUT 10 CM (4 IN.) LONG, SWIM DOWN RIVER TO THE OCEAN.

BETWEEN THEIR THIRD AND SIXTH YEAR IN SALT WATER THE SOCKEYE, NOW WEIGHING BETWEEN 2.5 KG (5 LBS.) AND 5.5 KG (12 LBS.), RETURN UN- ERRINGLY TO THE SPAWNING GROUND USED BY THEIR PARENTS. THUS THE SOCKEYE CYCLE BEGINS ANEW.

STEELHEAD

THE STEELHEAD IS A RAINBOW TROUT THAT SPENDS ITS ADULT LIFE IN SALT WATER, EXCEPT FOR SPAWNING. BECAUSE RAINBOW NEVER MIGRATE TO SALT WATER THEY RETAIN THE NAME, RAINBOW, ALTHOUGH IN THE KAMLOOPS REGION OF INTERIOR B.C. THEY ARE OFTEN CALLED KAMLOOPS TROUT. BOTH SPECIES CAN GROW TO 13.5 KG (30 LBS.) AND MORE.

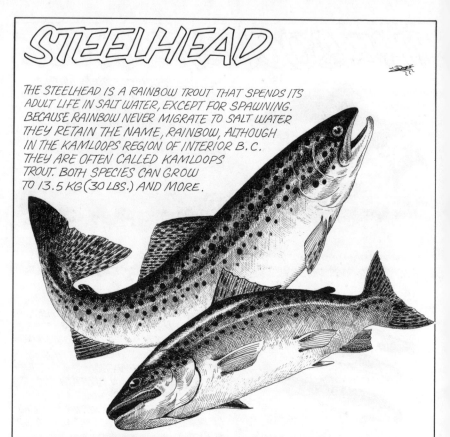

THE STEELHEAD'S COLOR VARIES ACCORDING TO ITS AGE AND LOCALITY. IT IS USUALLY DARK BLUE OR GREEN ON BACK AND UPPER SIDES, AND SILVER ON ITS LOWER SIDES AND BELLY. DISTINCT BLACK SPOTS SPECKLE ITS BACK, SIDES, TAIL, CAUDAL FIN, AND DORSAL FIN. DURING THE SPAWNING PERIOD A PINK OR REDDISH BAND RUNS LENGTHWISE ALONG ITS SIDE. THE STEELHEAD INHABITS MOST OF THE LARGER RIVERS AND THEIR TRIBUTARIES THAT EMPTY INTO THE PACIFIC. THE NON-MIGRATING RAINBOW IS FOUND IN THE FRASER, COLUMBIA AND PEACE RIVER SYSTEMS.

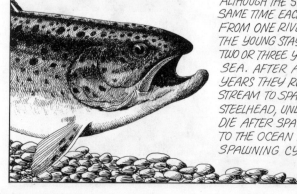

ALTHOUGH THE STEELHEAD SPAWNS AT THE SAME TIME EACH YEAR, THE TIME VARIES FROM ONE RIVER TO ANOTHER. MOST OF THE YOUNG STAY IN FRESH WATER FOR TWO OR THREE YEARS BEFORE GOING TO SEA. AFTER ANOTHER TWO OR THREE YEARS THEY RETURN TO THEIR HOME STREAM TO SPAWN IN GRAVEL AREAS. THE STEELHEAD, UNLIKE THE SALMON, DOES NOT DIE AFTER SPAWNING AND CAN RETURN TO THE OCEAN TO COMPLETE ANOTHER SPAWNING CYCLE.

BROOK TROUT

THE EASTERN BROOK TROUT, OR SPECKLED CHAR, HAS BEEN WIDELY INTRODUCED IN THE WEST WITH A GOOD DEGREE OF SUCCESS. TO BE AT ITS BEST, THE BROOK TROUT REQUIRES AN ENVIRONMENT THAT IS COLD AND CLEAR. IN SUCH A STREAM OR LAKE IT BECOMES TYPICAL OF THE RAINBOW TROUT SOUGHT AFTER AND ADMIRED BY ANGLERS. THE BROOK TROUT IS AN EXCITING AND COLORFUL GAME FISH THAT NOT ONLY GIVES ANGLERS A GOOD FIGHT BUT IS ALSO AN EXCELLENT TABLE FISH.

THE ADULT BROOK TROUT HAS BEAUTIFUL MARKINGS WHICH EASILY DISTINGUISH IT FROM ALL OTHER FISH. ITS BACK IS A DARK OLIVE-GREEN, RICHLY MARBLED WITH LIGHTER TONES. THE SIDES ARE MUCH LIGHTER AND SPRINKLED WITH YELLOW, BLUE AND RED SPOTS-- SOME RED SPOTS BEING RINGED WITH BLUE. THE FISH'S LOWER SIDES ARE PALE YELLOW WITH A LONGITUDINAL RED-ORANGE BAND. ITS BELLY IS NEARLY WHITE.

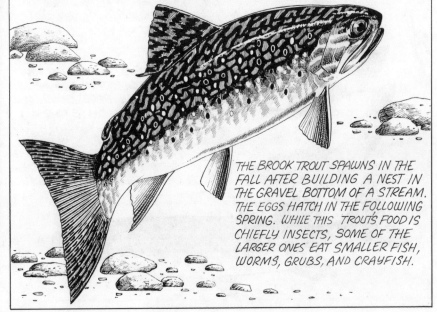

THE BROOK TROUT SPAWNS IN THE FALL AFTER BUILDING A NEST IN THE GRAVEL BOTTOM OF A STREAM. THE EGGS HATCH IN THE FOLLOWING SPRING. WHILE THIS TROUT'S FOOD IS CHIEFLY INSECTS, SOME OF THE LARGER ONES EAT SMALLER FISH, WORMS, GRUBS, AND CRAYFISH.

NORTHERN PIKE

THE NORTHERN PIKE, OR JACKFISH, IS A
RESIDENT OF CANADA'S NORTHERN LAKES
AND MUCH SOUGHT AFTER BY SPORTS
FISHERMEN. IT IS A LARGE FISH,
OFTEN REACHING A LENGTH WELL
OVER A METER (3 FT.) AND
WEIGHING UP TO 14 KG
(30 LBS.).

IT IS USUALLY GREEN OR BLUE-GREY
ON THE BACK AND SIDES, WITH
ORDERLY ROWS OF LIGHT SPOTS.

THE PIKE HAS AN ENORMOUS AP-
PETITE, DEVOURING GREAT QUANTI-
TIES OF SMALLER FISH AS WELL
AS INSECTS, YOUNG WATERFOWL,
AND OTHER ANIMAL LIFE. IN TURN
THE PIKE IS AN EXCELLENT FOOD
FISH AND, IN ADDITION, GIVES THE
SPORTS FISHERMAN A LIVELY
FIGHT.

THE PIKE SPAWNS EARLY IN SPRING.
THE YOUNG HATCH WITHIN TWO OR
THREE WEEKS AND GROW QUICKLY,
REACHING 20 TO 30 CM (8 TO 12 IN.)
BY AUTUMN.

SHARKS

SHOWN BELOW ARE THE SHARKS THAT INHABIT THE WATERS OF CANADA'S WEST COAST. SOME ARE RARELY SEEN, OTHERS ARE QUITE COMMON.

THE THRESHER SHARK, IN SPITE OF ITS LARGE SIZE OF 7.5M (25 FT.), IS NOT DANGEROUS TO MAN. ITS NAME COMES FROM ITS PRACTICE OF HERDING SCHOOLS OF SMALL FISH INTO MORE CONCENTRATED GROUPS BY THE THRESHING ACTION OF ITS LARGE TAIL.

THRESHER SHARK

SOUPFIN SHARK

A LENGTH OF 2M (6 FT.) IS ATTAINED BY THE SOUPFIN SHARK. SALMON, ROCKFISH, AND SQUID FORM THE LARGER PART OF ITS DIET. THE FINS OF THIS SHARK ARE HIGHLY PRIZED BY THE CHINESE WHO USE THEM IN SOUP.

BASKING SHARK

ALTHOUGH THE BASKING SHARK CAN GROW TO 13.5M (45 FT.) AND WEIGH 6 TONNES (5 TONS), IT IS NOT CONSIDERED DANGEROUS. IT LIVES ON PLANKTON WHICH IT OBTAINS BY STRAINING SEA WATER THROUGH ITS GILL RAKERS.

THE SEVENGILL SHARK IS A MEMBER OF THE COW SHARK FAMILY. IT DIFFERS FROM OTHER SHARKS IN THAT ITS DORSAL FIN IS FAR BACK ON ITS BODY.

SEVENGILL SHARK

SALMON SHARK
3M (10 FT.)

SIXGILL SHARK
7.5M (25 FT.)

BLUE SHARK
7.5M (25 FT.)

PACIFIC DOGFISH
1.5M (5 FT.)

BROWN CAT
.6M (2 FT.)

PACIFIC SLEEPER
7.5M (25 FT.)

DOGFISH

THE PACIFIC DOGFISH IS ABUNDANT ON CANADA'S
WEST COAST, ESPECIALLY WHERE HERRING SCHOOL.
IT ALSO FEEDS ON PILCHARDS, SMELTS, SAND-
LANCES, SQUID, AND CRUSTACEANS.
BECAUSE OF THIS VORACIOUS
APPETITE, IT IS A NUIS-
ANCE TO COMMERCIAL
AND SPORT FISHERMEN.

EARLIER IN WEST COAST HISTORY
THE DOGFISH WAS VALUED AS A
SOURCE OF OIL AND FERTILIZER.
IN 1940 SCIENTISTS DISCOVERED
A GOOD SOURCE OF VITAMIN A
IN THE DOGFISH LIVER AND FOR
ABOUT EIGHT YEARS IT WAS A
MUCH SOUGHT AFTER FISH.
WHEN SCIENTISTS LEARNED HOW
TO PRODUCE SYNTHETIC VITA-
MIN A, HOWEVER, THE DOGFISH
WAS NO LONGER OF COMMER-
CIAL VALUE.

WHILE THE DOGFISH IS NOT KNOWN AS A LONG DISTANCE
TRAVELER, ONE INDIVIDUAL TAGGED BY MARINE
BIOLOGISTS IN WASHINGTON STATE
WAS LATER CAPTURED 8,000 KM
(5,000 MILES) AWAY OFF
THE NORTHERN TIP OF
HONSHU ISLAND, JAPAN.

THE FEMALE DOGFISH IS
USUALLY LARGER AND
HEAVIER THAN THE
MALE AND MAY
GROW TO 1.5M (5 FT.).

RATFISH

LENGTH TO 1 M (3 FT.)

THE RATFISH IS QUITE COMMON ON THE PACIFIC COAST AND IS USUALLY FOUND AT DEPTHS OF 60M (200 FT.) OR MORE, ALTHOUGH IT IS OCCASIONALLY CAUGHT BY BOATS TROLLING FOR SALMON. SMALLER FISHES AND INVERTEBRATES FORM THE RATFISH'S DIET.

THIS ODD FISH DEPOSITS ITS EGGS IN LONG LEATHERY PURSES, SOMEWHAT LIKE THOSE OF SHARKS OR RAYS.

ALTHOUGH THE RATFISH IS A MEMBER OF THE CHIMERA FAMILY, IT HAS SOME OF THE CHARACTERISTICS OF BOTH THE SHARK AND THE BONY FISHES.

RATTAIL

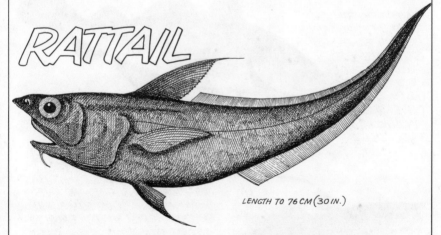

LENGTH TO 76 CM (30 IN.)

THE RATTAIL IS A CLOSE RELATIVE OF THE COD AND INHABITS DEEP WATERS ANYWHERE ALONG THE PACIFIC COAST. THE RATTAIL IS ONE OF THE MOST ABUNDANT FISHES OF THE DEEP SEAS. WHILE WE DO NOT CURRENTLY CONSIDER IT A FOOD FISH, AS OUR POPULATION GROWS AND SPECIES SUCH AS SALMON AND HALIBUT DECLINE,

WE MAY CHANGE OUR MINDS.

THE RATTAIL IS EASILY IDENTIFIED BY ITS TAPERED TAIL, POINTED NOSE AND UNDERSLUNG MOUTH. IT HAS AN AMAZING DEPTH TOLERANCE, INHABITING WATERS FROM 360M (1,200 FT.) TO NEARLY 3,000M (10,000 FT.).

COD

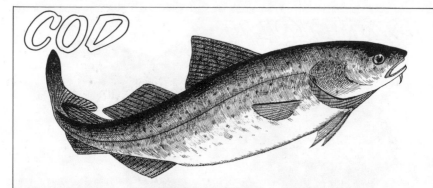

THIS IMPORTANT COMMERCIAL FISH INHABITS THE PACIFIC OCEAN ALL ALONG THE B.C. COAST. IT HAS RELATIVES IN THE ATLANTIC OCEAN WHICH ALSO ARE AN IMPORTANT PART OF THE COMMERCIAL FISHERY. COD IS AN EXCELLENT FOOD FISH, SOLD AS FROZEN FILLETS OR FISHSTICKS, AS WELL AS FRESH AND SMOKED.

THE PACIFIC COD, SHOWN ABOVE, GROWS TO 1M (3 FT.). THIS COD USUALLY FEEDS ON OR NEAR THE BOTTOM WHERE IT EATS SMALLER FISH SUCH AS HERRING AND VARIOUS CRUSTACEANS. THE PACIFIC COD MIGRATES FROM DEEP TO SHALLOW WATERS EACH SPRING AND SPAWNS IN LATE WINTER.

THE PACIFIC TOM COD, RIGHT, IS MUCH SMALLER THAN THE PACIFIC COD. IT USUALLY GROWS NO LONGER THAN 30 CM (12 IN.) AND IS OLIVE-GREEN WITH AN ALMOST WHITE UNDERSIDE.

THE LONGFIN COD, BELOW, IS NOT SO COMMON AND DIFFERS FROM THE OTHER COD IN TWO WAYS - - IT HAS ONLY TWO DORSAL FINS AND A VERY SHARP NOSE. IT IS USUALLY BLUISH OR GREENISH-GREY AND CAN GROW TO 46 CM (18 IN.).

SEAPERCH

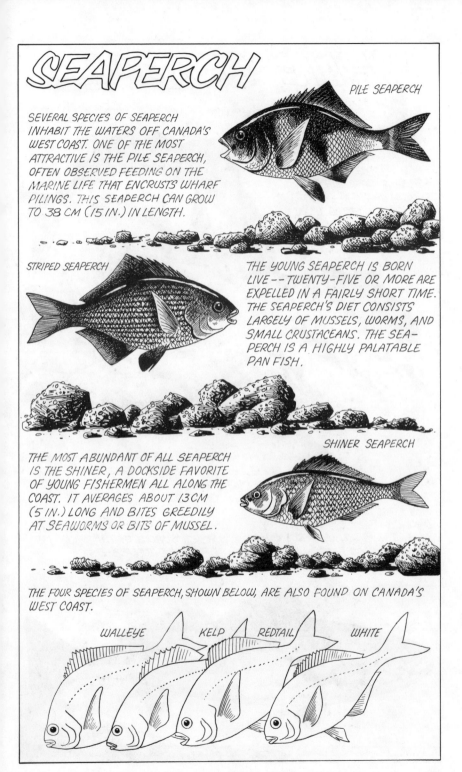

SEVERAL SPECIES OF SEAPERCH INHABIT THE WATERS OFF CANADA'S WEST COAST. ONE OF THE MOST ATTRACTIVE IS THE PILE SEAPERCH, OFTEN OBSERVED FEEDING ON THE MARINE LIFE THAT ENCRUSTS WHARF PILINGS. THIS SEAPERCH CAN GROW TO 38 CM (15 IN.) IN LENGTH.

PILE SEAPERCH

STRIPED SEAPERCH

THE YOUNG SEAPERCH IS BORN LIVE -- TWENTY-FIVE OR MORE ARE EXPELLED IN A FAIRLY SHORT TIME. THE SEAPERCH'S DIET CONSISTS LARGELY OF MUSSELS, WORMS, AND SMALL CRUSTACEANS. THE SEA-PERCH IS A HIGHLY PALATABLE PAN FISH.

THE MOST ABUNDANT OF ALL SEAPERCH IS THE SHINER, A DOCKSIDE FAVORITE OF YOUNG FISHERMEN ALL ALONG THE COAST. IT AVERAGES ABOUT 13 CM (5 IN.) LONG AND BITES GREEDILY AT SEAWORMS OR BITS OF MUSSEL.

SHINER SEAPERCH

THE FOUR SPECIES OF SEAPERCH, SHOWN BELOW, ARE ALSO FOUND ON CANADA'S WEST COAST.

WALLEYE   KELP   REDTAIL   WHITE

WHITE SEABASS

THE WHITE SEABASS IS A LARGE SILVERY FISH WITH A DARK BLUE OR BROWN BACK. ITS MOST RECOGNIZABLE FEATURE IS A DARK SPOT AT THE BASE OF EACH PECTORAL FIN. THE SEABASS CAN EXCEED A LENGTH OF 1.5 M (5 FT.) AND WEIGH MORE THAN 25 KG (55 LBS.).

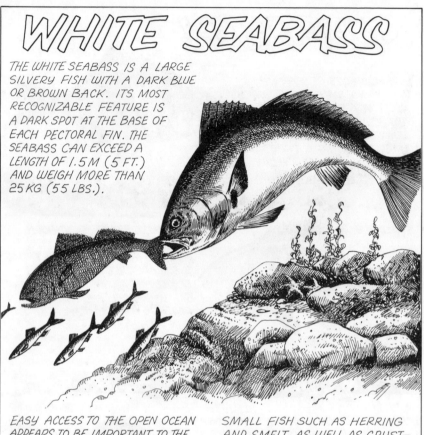

EASY ACCESS TO THE OPEN OCEAN APPEARS TO BE IMPORTANT TO THE SPECIES. IT IS OFTEN FOUND IN THE WATERS OF B.C.'S SOUTHERN COAST AND IS VERY ABUNDANT ON THE CALIFORNIA COAST, WHERE IT IS PRIZED AS A COMMERCIAL FOOD FISH AND AS A GAME FISH BY SPORTSMEN.

SMALL FISH SUCH AS HERRING AND SMELT, AS WELL AS CRUSTACEANS, ARE ITS MAIN SOURCE OF FOOD.

SPAWNING TAKES PLACE IN SUMMER, USUALLY IN THE VICINITY OF LARGE KELP BEDS.

ALBACORE

THE ALBACORE, LIKE THE TUNA, IS A MEMBER OF THE MACKEREL FAMILY. IT TRAVELS IN A SCHOOL AND IS A VERY FAST SWIMMER. ONLY YOUNG ALBACORE HAVE BEEN FOUND OFF CANADA'S WEST COAST, A FACT THAT LEADS MARINE BIOLOGISTS TO BELIEVE THAT THE ALBACORE IS A TROPICAL FISH WHOSE YOUNG RANGE NORTHWARD IN SEARCH OF FOOD AND RETURN TO THE TROPICS AS THEY MATURE. ITS FOOD CONSISTS OF A VARIETY OF HERRING-SIZE FISH, SQUID, AND SOMETIMES THE YOUNG OF ITS OWN SPECIES.

SINCE IT CAN GROW TO 3M (10 FT.) IN TROPICAL WATERS, THE ALBACORE IS SOUGHT AFTER BY SPORT AND COMMERCIAL FISHERMEN WHO SOMETIMES REFER TO IT AS THE LONGFIN TUNA.

TUNA

WHILE THE ALBACORE IS CAUGHT COMMERCIALLY OFF CANADA'S WEST COAST, THE TUNA IS SEEN ONLY RARELY, ALTHOUGH SEVERAL SPECIMENS HAVE BEEN RECORDED. THE TUNA IS CLOSELY RELATED TO THE ALBACORE -- THE LIFE HISTORY AND LIFE STYLE OF THE TWO FISH BEING SIMILAR. BOTH MAY RANGE 3,200 KM (2,000 MILES) TO 4,800 KM (3,000 MILES) IN QUEST OF FOOD.

BLUEFIN TUNA

SKIPJACK TUNA

ROCKFISH

QUILLBACK

THERE ARE AT LEAST TWENTY-FOUR SPECIES OF ROCKFISH IN THE WATERS OFF CANADA'S PACIFIC COAST. THEY VARY IN LENGTH FROM 19 CM (7½ IN.) TO 92 CM (36 IN.), AND ARE FOUND AT DEPTHS FROM 1M (3 FT.) TO MORE THAN 1,500M (4,800 FT.). THEY ALSO VARY WIDELY IN COLOR. THOSE IN TIDAL WATERS ARE USUALLY BROWN OR GREYISH, WHILE THOSE WHICH INHABIT GREATER DEPTHS TEND TO BE MORE VIVID. IN FACT, THEIR WIDE RANGE IN COLORATION IS EVIDENT IN THEIR NAMES -- BLUE, YELLOWTAIL, ORANGE, VERMILION, BLACKBLOTCHED, ROSY REDSTRIPE, GREENSTRIPE, BROWN, COPPER, RED SNAPPER, AND BLACK.

FLAG

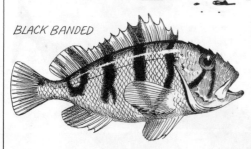

BLACK BANDED

LONG JAW

ROCKFISH ARE OFTEN ERRONE-OUSLY CALLED ROCKCOD, EVEN THOUGH THEY ARE NOT CLOSELY RELATED TO THE COD FAMILY. THEIR FLESH IS FIRM AND WHITE AND MAKES EXCELLENT FILLETS. FOR THIS REASON ROCK-FISH HAVE BECOME AN IMPORT-ANT PART OF THE PACIFIC COAST TRAWL AND SPORT FISHERY. ROCKFISH DIFFER FROM MANY FISH SPECIES IN THAT THE EGGS ARE FERTILIZED INTERNALLY AND THE YOUNG ARE BORN LIVE DURING THE SUMMER. THEY ARE ALMOST TRANSPARENT AND LESS THAN 1 CM (½ IN.) LONG. LIKE MANY OTHER SPECIES, THEY ARE BORN IN GREAT NUMBERS IN ORDER TO INSURE THAT SOME WILL SURVIVE THE SEA'S FOOD CHAIN.

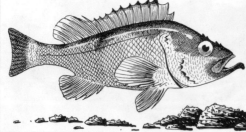

POACHERS

THE POACHER, OR SEAPOACHER, IS A BOTTOM DWELLER WITH THE AMAZING ABILITY TO LIVE AT DEPTHS FROM 18M (60 FT.) TO 1,100M (3,600 FT.). WHILE CERTAIN SPECIES OF POACHER ARE COMMON ON THE PACIFIC COAST, THEY ARE SELDOM SEEN EXCEPT WHEN CAUGHT IN THE TRAWLS OF COMMERCIAL FISHERMEN.

STURGEON POACHER

BLACKTIP POACHER

THE STURGEON POACHER, WHICH GROWS TO ABOUT 30CM (12 IN.), FEEDS LARGELY ON MARINE WORMS AND CRUSTACEANS.

THE BLACKTIP POACHER IS SMALLER, SOME 18CM (7 IN.) LONG, AND EASILY IDENTIFIED BY THE BLACK MARGIN ON ITS DORSAL FIN.

SMOOTH POACHER

THE SMOOTH POACHER IS NAMED BECAUSE OF A CONSPICUOUS LACK OF SPINES ON ITS ARMOR-PLATED BODY. IT GROWS TO 15 CM (6 IN.).

THE PYGMY POACHER, AS ITS NAME SUGGESTS, IS ONE OF THE SMALLEST POACHERS, GROWING TO ONLY 7.5 CM (3 IN.).

PYGMY POACHER

WOLF-EEL

THE MISNAMED WOLF-EEL OF CANADA'S PACIFIC COAST
IS NOT AN EEL BUT A MEMBER OF THE WOLF FISH
FAMILY. THERE ARE NO TRUE EELS ON THE
PACIFIC COAST. AN UGLY CREATURE, IT
IS OFTEN OVER 2M (6 FT.) LONG,
WITH A MOUTHFUL OF DOG-
LIKE TEETH, INCLUDING
MOLARS. ITS THICK
LIPS ARE COVERED
WITH WARTY
PROTUBERANCES.

THE WOLF-EEL CAN
BE BROWN, GREEN,
OR GREY, AND IS
LIBERALLY DECORATED
WITH LARGE DARK SPOTS.
IT DIFFERS FROM OTHER
FISH IN THAT IT HAS NO
PELVIC FINS.

THIS CREATURE'S DIET CONSISTS OF CRUSTACEANS,
SEA-URCHINS, CLAMS, MUSSELS, AND VARIOUS
KINDS OF FISH. IT IS VORACIOUS AND HAS
BEEN KNOWN TO ATTACK AND KILL FISH
ONLY SLIGHTLY SMALLER THAN ITSELF.
BY CONTRAST, IT CAN APPARENTLY
FAST FOR LONG PERIODS. CAPTIVE
SPECIMENS, FOR INSTANCE, HAVE
GONE EIGHT MONTHS AND MORE
WITHOUT EATING.

OCEAN ODDITIES

CANADA'S WEST COAST WATERS ARE
HOME TO MANY STRANGE CREATURES,
THE FOUR DESCRIBED HERE BEING
ONLY A FEW OF THE SPECIES
WHICH AT TIMES BORDER ON
THE UNBELIEVABLE.

ONE OF THE RAREST IS THE COSTER DORY,
RIGHT. THIS BIG-EYED FISH HAS BEEN
TAKEN ONLY ONCE ON OUR PACIFIC COAST.
A LARGE ONE WOULD MEASURE 18 CM (7 IN.) LONG.

THE SPINY LUMPSUCKER, LEFT, IS
FREQUENTLY CAUGHT BY SHRIMP
FISHERMEN IN THE WATERS OFF SOUTH-
ERN BRITISH COLUMBIA. THE
LUMPSUCKER HAS A SUCTION
DISC ON ITS BELLY AND IS
OFTEN FOUND ATTACHED TO A
ROCK. IT IS A SMALL FISH, SELDOM
REACHING 12.5 CM (5 IN.).

THE FOURHORN POACHER IS AN-
OTHER OF THE SMALLER
FISH, USUALLY MEAS-
URING LESS THAN
6.5 CM (2½ IN.). THE
POACHER'S BODY IS
FULLY ARMORED WITH A
SERIES OF BONY PLATES. IT IS
A BOTTOM DWELLER, ABLE TO LIVE
AT DEPTHS FROM TIDAL POOLS TO
OVER 106 M (360 FT.), USUALLY IN
THE COLD WATERS OF CANADA'S NORTH
PACIFIC COAST.

THE SAILFIN SCULPIN, OR SAILOR FISH, IS EASILY IDENTI-
FIED BY ITS TALL, SPINY DORSAL FIN. IT IS FAIRLY
COMMON IN THE WATERS OFF CANADA'S
SOUTHWEST COAST. THE
SAILFIN OCCASIONALLY
REACHES A LENGTH OF
20 CM (8 IN.). ITS FOOD
INCLUDES SHRIMPS AND
SMALL CRABS.

THE STOUT, LARGE-HEADED BOARFISH, RIGHT, IS USUALLY AN INHABITANT OF FAIRLY DEEP WATERS. IT MAY GROW TO 54 CM (22 IN.). THIS FISH HAS A DARK BROWN BACK, GRADUATING TO LIGHT BROWN ON THE BELLY, AND A RED HEAD.

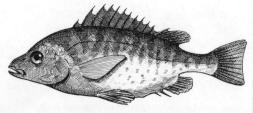

THE SEARCHER, LEFT, HAS AN EEL-LIKE BODY WITH A BROWN BACK AND BLACK MARKINGS. AN AID TO IDENTIFICATION IS THE BLACK SPOT ON THE FRONT OF THE DORSAL FIN. SEARCHERS GROW TO 30 CM (12 IN.).

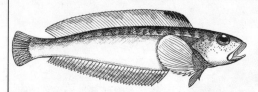

THE PACIFIC BONITO, RIGHT, REACHES A LENGTH OF 92 CM (36 IN.). IT HAS A DARK BLUE BACK WITH BLACK STRIPES AND A SILVER BELLY. IN ITS HOME WATERS OFF CALIFORNIA IT IS AN IMPORTANT SPORT FISH.

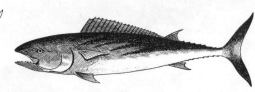

THE ROUGHEYE ROCKFISH, LEFT, HAS A RED BACK AND PINK SIDES WITH DARK BARS. IT MAY GROW TO 51 CM (20 IN.). THIS FISH AND SEVERAL OF ITS RELATIVES ARE OFTEN CALLED ROCK COD. THIS NAME IS A MISNOMER, HOWEVER, SINCE THE FISH IS NOT A COD.

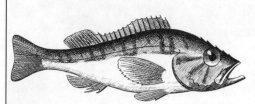

THE RIBBED SCULPIN, RIGHT, HAS A DARK OLIVE BACK WITH DARK BARS AND A WHITE BELLY. IT SELDOM GROWS LONGER THAN 18 CM (7 IN.). IT CAN BE DISTINGUISHED FROM OTHER MEMBERS OF THE SCULPIN FAMILY BY ITS SLENDER BODY.

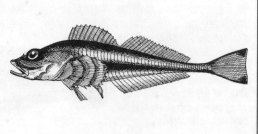

MARINE LIFE CHAIN

IN THE WATERS OF CANADA'S PACIFIC COAST, AS IN SALT WATERS THE WORLD OVER, THE DAILY QUEST FOR FOOD CREATES A NEVER ENDING CYCLE. WITHOUT FAIL EACH LIFE FORM EVENTUALLY BECOMES PART OF ANOTHER'S DIET IN THE FOOD CHAIN.

PLANT PLANKTON, SHOWN AT UPPER LEFT AND GREATLY MAGNIFIED, COMES IN THOUSANDS OF SHAPES AND SIZES AND IS EVIDENT IN EVERY DROP OF SEA WATER. MINUTE ANIMAL PLANKTON, SHOWN AT LEFT ALSO GREATLY MAGNIFIED, IS USUALLY THE LARVAE OF CRUSTACEANS, MARINE INSECTS, TINY FISH, AND WORMS. THEY FEED ON THE PLANT PLANKTON AND ARE, IN TURN, EATEN BY HERRING, PILCHARDS, AND FISH OF SIMILAR SIZE. THESE ARE PREYED UPON BY VARIOUS COD AND SALMON WHICH, IN TURN, BECOME FOOD FOR SHARKS, SEALS, AND OTHER LARGE SEA DWELLERS. WHEN A SHARK OR SEAL DIES, THE MINERALS RELEASED FROM ITS DECAYING BODY ARE ABSORBED BY THE PLANKTON, THUS COMPLETING THE CYCLE.

REPTILES

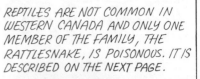

REPTILES ARE NOT COMMON IN WESTERN CANADA AND ONLY ONE MEMBER OF THE FAMILY, THE RATTLESNAKE, IS POISONOUS. IT IS DESCRIBED ON THE NEXT PAGE.

THE PAINTED TURTLE IS ABOUT 23 CM (9 IN.) LONG, OLIVE WITH RED AND YELLOW MARKINGS, AND INHABITS CANADA'S EXTREME SOUTH. ITS FOOD CONSISTS OF SMALL FISH, TADPOLES, SNAILS, AND SOME PLANT LIFE. THE FEMALE LAYS UP TO TWENTY EGGS IN A HOLE DUG IN THE GROUND NEAR THE POND OR LAKE THE TURTLE INHABITS.

THE WESTERN SKINK'S CHIEF SOURCE OF FOOD APPEARS TO BE INSECTS. THIS SKINK IS ABOUT 14 CM (5½ IN.) LONG, BROWNISH-OLIVE AND USUALLY FOUND IN DAMP AREAS AND IN WELL ROTTED WOOD. THREE OR FOUR EGGS ARE LAID AT A TIME WITH THE FEMALE ATTENDING THEM UNTIL THEY HATCH. THE YOUNG HAVE BLUE TAILS.

THE NORTHERN ALLIGATOR LIZARD GROWS TO 25 CM (10 IN.). IT IS USUALLY GREY OR BROWN WITH DARK SPOTS.

DRY ROCKY AREAS ARE HOME TO THIS REPTILE AND, LIKE THE SKINK, ITS FOOD IS MAINLY INSECTS, THUS BENEFITING MAN. WHEN GRABBED BY THE TAIL THIS LIZARD PROMPTLY SHEDS IT AND ESCAPES. LOSS OF ITS TAIL IS A MINOR INCONVENIENCE, HOWEVER, SINCE IT SOON GROWS A NEW ONE. THE FEMALE GIVES LIVE BIRTH TO FOUR OR FIVE YOUNG.

THE RUBBER SNAKE, OR RUBBER BOA, IS EASILY IDENTIFIED BY ITS SHORT THICK SHAPE, EVEN BROWN COLORING AND SLOW MOVEMENT. IT GROWS TO 76 CM (30 IN.). IT IS BELIEVED THAT THE RUBBER SNAKE SPENDS A GOOD DEAL OF TIME UNDER-GROUND, USUALLY IN THE BURROWS OF MICE, MOLES, AND OTHER SMALL CREATURES WHICH FORM THE MAIN PART OF ITS DIET.

RATTLESNAKE

THE NORTHERN PACIFIC RATTLESNAKE IS FOUND IN THE INTERIOR DRY BELT OF BRITISH COLUMBIA, AS WELL AS IN SOUTHERN ALBERTA AND SASKATCHEWAN. IT GROWS TO 1.5 M (5 FT.) BUT ON AVERAGE IS USUALLY HALF THAT SIZE. THIS REPTILE IS CAPABLE OF INFLICTING A SEVERE WOUND WHICH CAN PROVE FATAL. ITS COLOR RANGES FROM OLIVE-GREY TO BROWN, WITH DARK BROWN SPOTS RINGED WITH NEAR WHITE. IT IS, FORTUNATELY, NOT AN AGGRESSIVE SNAKE AND UNLESS FRIGHTENED OR TEASED WILL OFFER NO TROUBLE. IT USUALLY HIBER-NATES IN LARGE GROUPS DURING THE WINTER.

A LARGER, LESS COLOR-FUL RATTLESNAKE, THE PRAIRIE RATTLESNAKE, IS FOUND IN SOUTHERN ALBERTA AND SASK-ATCHEWAN.

RATTLESNAKE RATTLE   CROSS—SECTION

WHEN THE RATTLESNAKE VIBRATES ITS TAIL MUSCLES, THE HORNY SEGMENTS PRODUCE A RATTLING SOUND WHICH GIVES THE SNAKE ITS NAME.

WHEN THE RATTLER'S JAWS ARE CLOSED, ITS VENOM-INJECTING FANGS REST AGAINST THE ROOF OF ITS MOUTH. A FANG IS EXPENDABLE AND IF BRO-KEN IS REPLACED BY ONE FROM A CAPSULE BEHIND THE EXISTING FANG. THE PLACEMENT OF ITS WINDPIPE OPENING ENABLES THE RATTLER TO BREATH DURING THE PROCESS OF SWALLOWING ITS PREY.

THE NORTHERN PACIFIC RATTLER IS A MEMBER OF THE PIT VIPER FAMILY, SO NAMED BECAUSE OF THE SENSORY PIT BEHIND ITS NOSTRIL. THE PIT ENABLES THE SNAKE TO SEEK OUT AND STRIKE WARM-BLOODED PREY EVEN IN TOTAL DARKNESS. IN EFFECT, IT PROVIDES THE RATTLER WITH A SIXTH SENSE.

THE LARGE NUMBER OF RODENTS DE-STROYED BY THIS SNAKE GIVE IT SOME DEGREE OF ECONOMIC VALUE.

SHOWN BELOW ARE THE MAIN ITEMS CONSUMED BY THE NORTHERN PACIFIC RATTLER

MICE   GOPHERS   CHIPMUNKS   SMALL BIRDS

HARMLESS SNAKES

IN CANADA THE GOPHER SNAKE, RIGHT, IS FOUND ONLY IN THE DRIER AREAS OF SOUTHERN BRITISH COLUMBIA. IT IS A DIRTY YELLOW COLOR WITH DARK SPOTS, AND CAN GROW TO JUST UNDER 2M (6FT.). ITS ABILITY TO DESTROY AND DEVOUR GREAT NUMBERS OF GOPHERS AND MICE MAKE IT POPULAR WITH CROP-GROWING FARMERS.

THE BLUE RACER, LEFT, GETS ITS NAME FROM AN ABILITY TO STREAK ACROSS THE GROUND AT A SPEED THAT MAKES IT ALMOST IMPOSSIBLE TO CATCH. IT INHABITS MUCH THE SAME RANGE AS THE GOPHER SNAKE, AND LIVES ON INSECTS, MICE, AND BIRDS' EGGS. IF CORNERED THE BLUE RACER MAY TURN ON ITS ATTACKER BUT ITS BITE IS NOT POISONOUS. IT CAN GROW TO OVER 1M (3FT.).

THE STRIPED, OR NORTHWESTERN GARTER SNAKE, SHOWN AT RIGHT, CAN REACH A LENGTH OF 1M (3FT.). ITS COLORATION IS GENERALLY DARK WITH THREE STRIPES RUNNING FROM HEAD TO TAIL. THE COLORS OF THE STRIPES VARY FROM BLUE TO GREY, YELLOW OR GREEN. EXCEPT FOR NORTHERN REGIONS, THIS SNAKE RANGES THROUGH WESTERN CANADA. IT IS A GOOD SWIMMER AND, WHEN LIVING NEAR WATER, FEEDS ON SMALL FISH, FROGS, TADPOLES, AND INSECTS.

THE COAST GARTER SNAKE, BELOW, CAN GROW SLIGHTLY LONGER THAN 1M (3FT.). IT IS USUALLY QUITE DARK WITH A YELLOW STRIPE DOWN ITS BACK. THIS STRIPE IS BROKEN BY DARK SPOTS ON EACH SIDE. THE COAST GARTER SNAKE IS FOUND NEAR BEACHES, SELDOM FAR FROM THE WATER. IT IS AGGRESSIVE AND WHILE IT MAY STRIKE VICIOUSLY WHEN CORNERED OR TEASED, IT IS NOT POISONOUS. IT FEEDS ON SMALL FISH, TADPOLES, INSECTS, AND WORMS.

LEOPARD FROG

THE LEOPARD FROG IS, WITHOUT DOUBT, ONE OF CANADA'S HANDSOMEST AMPHIBIANS. IT GROWS TO ABOUT 10 CM (4 IN.) AND COMES IN SHADES OF GREY, BROWN, OR GREEN, WITH LARGE DARK SPOTS. THE COLORS AND MARKINGS ARE HIGHLY VARIABLE, HOWEVER, AND MAY DIFFER FROM ONE POND OR SWAMP TO THE NEXT. CONSEQUENTLY, SOME SCIENTISTS BELIEVE THERE ARE SEVERAL SUBSPECIES, WHILE OTHERS ARGUE THERE IS ONLY ONE SPECIE.

THE LEOPARD FROG IS FOUND THROUGHOUT CANADA WITH THE EXCEPTION OF THE PACIFIC COAST AND THE FAR NORTHERN REGIONS. IT INHABITS SWAMPS AND PONDS IN THE SPRING AND TURNS TO GRASSY FOREST FLOORS IN THE SUMMER. THIS FROG IS ALSO KNOWN AS THE MEADOW FROG BECAUSE OF ITS WANDERING FAR AWAY FROM WATER.

THIS COLORFUL FROG IS OFTEN USED IN LABORATORY EXPERIMENTS. IF LEFT ALONE IT CAN LIVE EIGHT YEARS OR MORE.

TREE-TOADS

SEVERAL VARIETIES OF TREE-TOADS, OR TREE-FROGS, MAY BE FOUND IN ONE LOCALE OR ANOTHER ACROSS SOUTHERN CANADA. TREE-TOADS ARE TINY — NEVER MORE THAN 2.5 CM (1 IN.) TO 4.5 (1¾ IN.) IN LENGTH. THEIR COLOR MAY VARY FROM BROWN, BRONZE, GREEN, GREY, TO BUFF. THEY ARE, TO SOME EXTENT, CAPABLE OF CHANGING THEIR COLOR TO MATCH THEIR ENVIRONMENT.

THE TREE-TOADS' FINGERS AND TOES END IN ROUND PADS THAT ENABLE THEM TO CLIMB ALMOST ANYWHERE IN SEARCH OF THEIR INSECT FOOD, WHICH THEY CATCH WITH THEIR STICKY TONGUES.

IN SPRING THE TREE-TOADS GATHER IN PONDS AND SWAMPS TO FORM NOISY CHORUSES. ONLY THE MALES CROAK. WHILE BURSTING FORTH IN SONG THEIR THROAT MEMBRANES MAY SWELL TO THREE TIMES THE SIZE OF THEIR HEADS.

TREE-TOADS LAY EGGS THROUGHOUT THE SPRINGTIME IN MILDER AREAS BUT NOT UNTIL JUNE OR JULY IN COOLER REGIONS.

SALAMANDERS

MOST SALAMANDERS BEGIN LIFE IN WATER WHERE THEY HATCH FROM EGGS SIMILAR TO THOSE OF THE FROG. SINCE SALAMANDERS CANNOT LIVE IN AREAS THAT ARE SUNNY AND DRY, THEY INHABIT PONDS, LAKES, RIVERS, CREEKS, AND SWAMPS, OR DANK PLACES UNDER LOGS OR ROCKS.

SALAMANDERS VARY GREATLY IN SIZE. THE SMALLEST, FROM THE SOUTHEASTERN UNITED STATES, IS ONLY 5CM (2 IN.) LONG, WHILE THE GIANT SALAMANDER OF THE ORIENT CAN GROW TO OVER 3M (10 FT.). THE SALAMANDERS OF WESTERN CANADA RANGE BETWEEN 11CM (4½ IN.) AND 30CM (12 IN.) LONG.

TIGER SALAMANDER

PACIFIC COAST NEWT

PACIFIC GIANT SALAMANDER

AN UNUSUAL FEATURE OF THE SALAMANDERS IS THE VARIETY OF WAYS THEY BREATHE. WHILE IN THE LARVAL STAGE THEY ALL USE GILLS FOR BREATHING. AS ADULTS, SOME SPECIES HAVE LUNGS, WHILE SOME HAVE FISH-LIKE GILLS. OTHERS HAVE NEITHER. THEY GET THEIR OXYGEN THROUGH THEIR SKIN BY EXTRACTING IT FROM THE MOISTURE THAT IS SO IMPORTANT TO THEM. ALL SALAMANDERS, HOWEVER, ALWAYS HAVE MOIST SKIN LIKE THAT OF FROGS.

SALAMANDERS LIVE ON INSECTS, WORMS, AND SIMILAR SMALL CREATURES, WHILE THEMSELVES FALLING PREY TO HOUSE CATS, FOXES, CROWS AND OTHER PREDATORS.

NORTHWESTERN SALAMANDER

BRITISH COLUMBIA SALAMANDER

WESTERN RED-BACKED SALAMANDER

LONG-TOED SALAMANDER

114

POND INSECTS

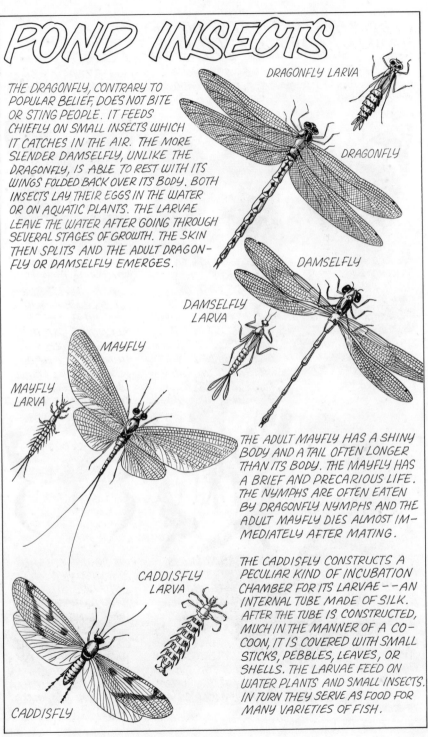

THE DRAGONFLY, CONTRARY TO POPULAR BELIEF, DOES NOT BITE OR STING PEOPLE. IT FEEDS CHIEFLY ON SMALL INSECTS WHICH IT CATCHES IN THE AIR. THE MORE SLENDER DAMSELFLY, UNLIKE THE DRAGONFLY, IS ABLE TO REST WITH ITS WINGS FOLDED BACK OVER ITS BODY. BOTH INSECTS LAY THEIR EGGS IN THE WATER OR ON AQUATIC PLANTS. THE LARVAE LEAVE THE WATER AFTER GOING THROUGH SEVERAL STAGES OF GROWTH. THE SKIN THEN SPLITS AND THE ADULT DRAGONFLY OR DAMSELFLY EMERGES.

DRAGONFLY LARVA

DRAGONFLY

DAMSELFLY

DAMSELFLY LARVA

MAYFLY

MAYFLY LARVA

THE ADULT MAYFLY HAS A SHINY BODY AND A TAIL OFTEN LONGER THAN ITS BODY. THE MAYFLY HAS A BRIEF AND PRECARIOUS LIFE. THE NYMPHS ARE OFTEN EATEN BY DRAGONFLY NYMPHS AND THE ADULT MAYFLY DIES ALMOST IMMEDIATELY AFTER MATING.

THE CADDISFLY CONSTRUCTS A PECULIAR KIND OF INCUBATION CHAMBER FOR ITS LARVAE -- AN INTERNAL TUBE MADE OF SILK. AFTER THE TUBE IS CONSTRUCTED, MUCH IN THE MANNER OF A COCOON, IT IS COVERED WITH SMALL STICKS, PEBBLES, LEAVES, OR SHELLS. THE LARVAE FEED ON WATER PLANTS AND SMALL INSECTS. IN TURN THEY SERVE AS FOOD FOR MANY VARIETIES OF FISH.

CADDISFLY LARVA

CADDISFLY

BUTTERFLIES

THESE COLORFUL CREATURES OF BRIGHT SUMMER DAYS ARE FOUND THROUGHOUT WESTERN CANADA'S PRAIRIES, ALPINE MEADOWS, SALTWATER MARSHES, FORESTS, AND GARDENS.

THE RED ADMIRAL IS COMMON ALL OVER THE NORTHERN HEMISPHERE. IT IS EASILY IDENTIFIED BY THE RED BANDS ON ITS DARK BROWN WINGS WHICH USUALLY HAVE A SPREAD OF CLOSE TO 5CM (2 IN.).

YELLOW BANDS AND BLUE SPOTS ON THE OUTSIDE EDGE OF BROWN WINGS ARE THE MOURNING CLOAK'S IDENTIFICATION MARKS. WHILE ONLY ONE BATCH OF EGGS IS LAID IN THE NORTH, IN WARMER CLIMATES TWO BATCHES A YEAR ARE NORMAL.

THE COMMON WOOD NYMPH IS IDENTIFIED BY ITS DULL BROWN WINGS WITH A PAIR OF YELLOW PATCHES SURROUNDING PURPLE SPOTS ON EACH FOREWING. IN CANADA NYMPHS ARE FOUND MOSTLY IN OPEN FORESTS AND MOUNTAIN AREAS.

THE CABBAGE BUTTERFLY IS A COMMON PEST THAT CAME TO NORTH AMERICA IN 1868 AND IN ONLY TWENTY YEARS SPREAD OVER THE ENTIRE CONTINENT. TWO OR THREE BROODS ARE HATCHED EACH YEAR. THIS INSECT'S WING SPAN IS 5CM (2 IN.).

THE SWALLOWTAIL IS OUR MOST BEAUTIFUL AND LARGEST BUTTERFLY, ITS VIVID BLACK AND YELLOW WINGS HAVING A SPAN OF ALMOST 10 CM (4 IN.). FEW CAN OVERLOOK THE BEAUTY OF THIS INSECT AS IT FLUTTERS ABOUT ON A SUMMER'S DAY.

THE ORANGE SULPHUR IS SOMETIMES PALE, BUT MORE USUALLY BRIGHT ORANGE WITH DARK WING TIPS. THIS BUTTERFLY IS QUITE COMMON IN GARDENS AND MEADOWS, ITS LARVAE FEEDING MAINLY ON CLOVER, ALFALFA, PEAS, AND OTHER LEGUMES.

MOTHS

WHILE MOTHS ARE BLAMED FOR UNTOLD DAMAGE TO VEGETABLES, SHRUBS, AND TREES, IT IS WHILE THEY ARE IN THE CATERPILLAR, OR LARVAE, STAGE THAT THEY DO THEIR DESTRUCTIVE WORK.

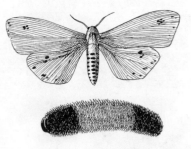

THE TOMATO HORNWORM IS THE LARVA OF ONE VARIETY OF SPHINX MOTH, OF WHICH THERE ARE CLOSE TO 100 SPECIES IN NORTH AMERICA. IT FEEDS ON SUCH THINGS AS TOMATOES, POTATOES, SHRUBS AND TREES, OFTEN DOING SEVERE DAMAGE IF LEFT UNCHECKED. HOWEVER, THE HORN AT THE END OF THE LARVA IS NOT POISONOUS––AS MANY PEOPLE BELIEVE.

THE WOOLLY BEAR CATERPILLAR, COMMON IN FALL AND A LONG TIME FAVORITE OF CHILDREN, IS THE LARVA OF THE ISABELLA MOTH. IT FEEDS MOSTLY ON PLANTAIN AND SIMILAR GROWTH. THE ISABELLA, A MEDIUM SIZE MOTH MEASURING SOME 5CM (2 IN.) ACROSS, IS A COPPERY-BUFF COLOR WITH A FEW DARK SPOTS.

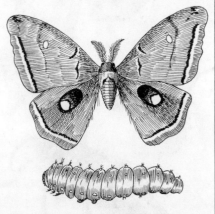

THE FALL CANKERWORM IS A THREAT TO FRUIT ORCHARDS AND WITHOUT PROPER CONTROL CAN DO GREAT DAMAGE. THE FEMALE IS WINGLESS AND LAYS ITS EGGS IN THE BARK OF A TREE. THE LARVA FEEDS ON THE LEAVES, HENCE ITS POTENTIAL TO DAMAGE TREES.

THE POLYPHEMUS MOTH IS WESTERN CANADA'S LARGEST, USUALLY MEASURING MORE THAN 12.5CM (5 IN.) ACROSS. ITS LARGE GREEN LARVA FEEDS MAINLY ON TREES AND SHRUBS.

HORNET

THE HORNET IS UNIQUE IN THAT WHILE AN ADULT LIVES ON NECTAR AND FRUIT JUICES, THE LARVA IS CARNIVOROUS. THE ADULT MUST THEREFORE GATHER GREAT NUMBERS OF FLIES AND CATERPILLARS — A BENEFIT TO MAN BECAUSE THIS ACTIVITY HELPS KEEP THESE PESTS UNDER CONTROL.

THE HORNET'S NEST IS CONSTRUCTED OF PAPER MANUFACTURED FROM WOOD FIBERS. THE NESTS ARE BUILT IN VARIOUS SIZES, WITH THE LARGER ONES HAVING A POPULATION OF SEVERAL THOUSAND. FER-TILIZED EGGS BECOME WORK-ERS OR QUEENS, DEPENDING ON THE KIND OF NOURISH-MENT THEY RECEIVE. THE UNFERTILIZED EGGS DEVELOP INTO DRONES, OR MALES.

FRUIT PICKERS, FISHER-MEN, BEE-KEEPERS, AND PICNICKERS HAVE ALL BEEN PLAGUED BY THIS AGGRESS-IVE INSECT IN ITS RELENT-LESS SEARCH FOR FOOD. HUMANS, AS WELL AS LESSER ANIMALS, HAVE BEEN STUNG TO DEATH BY ANGRY HORNETS.

STARFISH

THE STARFISH IS PROTECTED BY A ROUGH SPINY SKIN. ON TOP OF THE ANIMAL IS A SIEVE PLATE. WATER PASSES THROUGH THIS PLATE AND ALONG CANALS TO ITS TUBE FEET WHICH ARE SUCKER-LIKE APPENDAGES ON THE UNDERSIDE OF ITS ARMS. FOR THIS REASON, PULLING A STARFISH FROM A ROCK CAN BE QUITE DIFFICULT.

THE PURPLE, OR OCHRE, STARFISH IS THE ONE MOST COMMONLY SEEN ON CANADA'S WEST COAST AT LOW TIDE. IT IS ABOUT 23CM (9 IN.) ACROSS BUT CAN GROW MUCH LARGER.

THE MOTTLED STARFISH IS USUALLY LARGER AND HAS NARROW ARMS. AS THE NAME SUGGESTS, IT IS MOTTLED BROWN OR GREEN AND GROWS TO 61 CM (24 IN.) IN DIAMETER.

THE SUNFLOWER STARFISH IS ONE OF THE LARGEST IN THE WORLD, ATTAINING A BREADTH OF 81CM (32 IN.). IT IS USUALLY PINK BUT OTHER COLORS DO OCCUR.

WHILE THE STARFISH IS CONSIDERED TO BE ONE OF THE LOWER ANIMALS, IT HAS AN ABILITY THAT WE HIGHER ANIMALS MIGHT WELL ENVY. WHEN, THROUGH SOME MISHAP, IT LOSES AN ARM, IT GROWS A NEW ONE.

CLAMS AND OYSTERS ARE A LARGE PART OF THE STARFISH'S DIET. IT USES SUCTION TO FORCE THE BIVALVE OPEN AND EXTENDS ITS STOMACH INTO THE VICTIM.

THE SEA URCHIN IS CLOSELY RELATED TO THE STARFISH. IT LACKS ARMS BUT HAS THE SAME STAR-SHAPED BODY PLAN.

THE SAND DOLLAR, TOO, IS A RELATIVE OF THE STARFISH. IT IS FLAT, CIRCULAR, AND VELVETY TO THE TOUCH. IT GROWS UP TO 7CM (3 IN.) ACROSS.

CRABS

THE EDIBLE CRAB, RIGHT, GROWS AS LARGE AS 25 CM (10 IN.) ACROSS THE SHELL. IT IS BROWN TO PURPLE IN COLOR, BECOMING RED ONLY WHEN COOKED. LIKE MOST CRABS, IT IS GENERALLY FOUND ON SANDY BOTTOMS NEAR UNDERWATER VEGETATION AND IS VERY FOND OF CLAMS.

EDIBLE CRAB

ROCK CRAB

THE ROCK CRAB USUALLY INHABITS ROCKY BOTTOMS. IT IS MAROON, OFTEN WITH BLACK CLAWS. LIKE ALL TRUE CRABS, IT HAS ONE PAIR OF PINCERS AND FOUR PAIRS OF WALKING LEGS. THE ROCK CRAB GROWS TO 20 CM (8 IN.) ACROSS THE SHELL. SINCE CRABS HAVE AN EXOSKELETON, THEY GROW BY MOULTING. EACH TIME IT CASTS OFF ITS OLD SHELL, IT HIDES UNTIL MATERIAL IT EXCRETES HARDENS TO FORM A NEW SHELL.

PURPLE SHORE CRAB

HAIRY HERMIT CRAB

GRANULAR HERMIT CRAB

THERE ARE MANY BEACHES ON THE PACIFIC COAST WHERE THERE ARE ONE OR MORE SMALL CRABS UNDER EVERY ROCK. THESE LITTLE CRUSTACEANS ARE KNOWN AS PURPLE SHORE CRABS. THEY SELDOM GROW LARGER THAN 4 CM (1½ IN.) ACROSS THE SHELL. HAIRY SHORE CRABS WITH THEIR HAIR-FRINGED LEGS ARE ALMOST AS NUMEROUS.

THE HAIRY HERMIT CRAB CAN GROW TO 5 CM (2 IN.) ACROSS THE SHELL. IT PREFERS TO HOUSE ITSELF IN AN ABANDONED SEA SHELL THAT IS LARGE ENOUGH TO ALLOW FREEDOM OF MOVEMENT. IT IS SEEN FREQUENTLY IN SHALLOW WATER AND IN TIDAL POOLS.

THE GRANULAR HERMIT CRAB IS NAMED FOR THE GRANULAR TEXTURE OF ITS PINCERS. IT ALSO MEASURES 5 CM (2 IN.). THIS CRAB ALSO CARRIES WITH IT AN ABANDONED SEA SHELL LARGE ENOUGH TO BACK INTO FOR PROTECTION.

OCTOPUS

THERE ARE MANY SPECIES OF OCTOPI,
SOME NO LONGER THAN 2.5CM (1IN.),
ALTHOUGH ONE SPECIES IN THE
NORTH PACIFIC GROWS LONGER
THAN 7.5M (25 FT.). THE
MAJORITY, HOWEVER, ARE
VERY SMALL AND AB-
SOLUTELY HARMLESS
TO MAN. THESE
MOLLUSKS WILL
OFTEN CHANGE COLOR
WHEN EXCITED OR SCARED.
IN ADDITION, THEY CAN STAIN
THE SURROUNDING WATER WITH A
DENSE, INKY FLUID --AN EFFECTIVE
METHOD OF DEFENCE. ONE OF THE MAIN
ITEMS IN THE OCTOPUS' DIET IS CRAB.

THE OCTOPUS IS ABLE TO CRAWL
ALONG THE SEA BOTTOM USING
ITS ARMS, OR IT CAN EJECT A
STREAM OF WATER AND JET-PROPEL
ITSELF AS SHOWN AT LEFT.

THE FEMALE LAYS HER EGGS IN
JELLY-LIKE BUNCHES ON PRO-
TECTED ROCKS, THEN GUARDS HER
EGGS UNTIL THEY ARE HATCHED.

SQUID

THE SQUID, UNLIKE ITS RELATIVE THE OCTOPUS, IS
OFTEN FOUND IN LARGE SCHOOLS. IT HAS TEN
ARMS, OR TENTACLES, TWO OF WHICH ARE
LONGER AND HAVE SPADE-LIKE EXTREMITIES
FOR GRASPING ITS PREY. THE EIGHT SHORTER
ARMS ARE USED FOR PUSHING FOOD INTO ITS
ARMORED BEAK.

LIKE THE OCTOPUS, THE SQUID CAN EJECT INKY
FLUID FROM A GLAND AS A DEFENCE MECH-
ANISM. SQUID RANGE IN SIZE FROM 23CM
(9 IN.) TO 14 M (45 FT.).

CLAMS

THE PACIFIC COAST IS HOME FOR SEVERAL SPECIES OF CLAMS, OF WHICH THE BUTTER CLAM IS THE MOST PLENTIFUL. IT IS USED COMMERCIALLY AND ITS AVAILABILITY MADE IT A STAPLE OF COASTAL NATIVES FOR HUNDREDS OF YEARS. HOWEVER, PEOPLE WHO ENJOY CLAM CHOWDER AND HAVE VISIONS OF DIGGING THEIR OWN CLAMS SHOULD REMEMBER THAT THE NICE BIG ONES HIDE DEEP IN THE SAND AND ARE DIFFICULT TO CAPTURE -- EVEN WITH A "CLAM GUN," AS A CLAM DIGGING SHOVEL IS CALLED.

CLAMS LIVE IN A HARD, HINGED SHELL AND MOVE BY MEANS OF A MUSCULAR FOOT WHICH IS EXTENDED FROM THE SHELL. THEY EAT MICROSCOPIC FOOD WHICH, WITH OXYGEN, IS TAKEN IN BY A SYPHON. ANOTHER SYPHON EXPELS WATER AND WASTE MATERIALS. THE CLAM'S SHELL IS CONSTRUCTED OF LIME FROM A SOFT MEMBRANE CALLED A "MANTLE." THE RIDGES ON THE SHELL, WHILE DECORATIVE IN APPEARANCE, ARE ACTUALLY GROWTH RINGS.

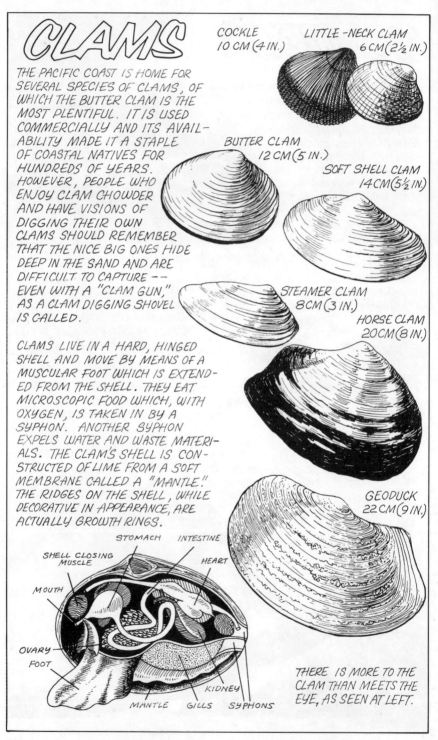

COCKLE
10 CM (4 IN.)

LITTLE-NECK CLAM
6 CM (2½ IN.)

BUTTER CLAM
12 CM (5 IN.)

SOFT SHELL CLAM
14 CM (5½ IN.)

STEAMER CLAM
8 CM (3 IN.)

HORSE CLAM
20 CM (8 IN.)

GEODUCK
22 CM (9 IN.)

STOMACH INTESTINE

SHELL CLOSING MUSCLE

HEART

MOUTH

OVARY

FOOT

KIDNEY

MANTLE GILLS SYPHONS

THERE IS MORE TO THE CLAM THAN MEETS THE EYE, AS SEEN AT LEFT.

CAMPSITE VISITORS

PEOPLE ARE NOT THE ONLY VISITORS TO WESTERN CANADA'S BEAUTIFUL CAMPSITES. MANY CREATURES OF THE FOREST AND FIELD HAVE LEARNED TO TAKE ADVANTAGE OF THE CRUMBS AND SCRAPS LEFT BY CAMPERS. BECAUSE OF THEIR CONSTANT ASSOCIATION WITH THE HUMAN ELEMENT, SOME OF THESE CREATURES ARE QUITE TAME, WHILE OTHERS ARE DOWNRIGHT IMPUDENT!

THE RED SQUIRREL IS A VISITOR TO CAMPSITES THAT ARE AMONG CONIFEROUS TREES. WHEN NOT SCROUNGING FOOD FROM CAMPERS IT FEEDS ON SEEDS OF CONE-BEARING TREES OR BUDS FROM OTHER TREES. THE RED SQUIRREL BREEDS IN APRIL, WITH UP TO SIX YOUNG BORN IN EARLY JUNE.

THERE ARE SEVERAL SPECIES OF CHIPMUNK IN WESTERN CANADA. ONE OR ANOTHER OF THEM IS LIKELY TO BE A VISITOR TO ALMOST ANY CAMPSITE. ASIDE FROM HANDOUTS, IT EATS SEEDS AND BERRIES WHICH IT STORES IN LARGE AMOUNTS IN ITS TINY BURROW.

THE MAGPIE IS A STRIKING BLACK AND WHITE BIRD THAT OFTEN GLIDES, RATHER THAN FLIES, FROM TREE TO TREE.

THE CANADA JAY, OR WHISKY JACK AS IT IS COMMONLY CALLED, IS THE SASSIEST OF ALL CAMPSITE VISITORS. IT WILL SIT ON A PICNIC TABLE SNATCHING WHAT-EVER FOOD IT CAN REACH AND OFTEN BECOMES TAME ENOUGH TO HAND FEED.

BEAKS for EVERYTHING

THE BEAKS OF DIFFERENT SPECIES OF BIRDS HAVE EVOLVED TO SUIT THEIR DIFFERENT METHODS OF OBTAINING FOOD. THE HERON, FOR INSTANCE, HAS A STRONG SHARPLY POINTED BEAK THAT EN-ABLES IT TO SPEAR FISH.

HAWKS, OWLS, AND EAGLES ARE ENDOWED WITH BEAKS THAT ENABLE THEM TO TEAR FLESH EASILY.

SNIPE AND OTHER SHORE-BIRDS HAVE BEAKS ADAPTED TO PROBING IN MUD. THE WARBLER'S BEAK IS DESIGNED FOR PICKING UP INSECTS. BY CONTRAST, THE DUCK'S BILL HAS TOOTH-LIKE PLATES THROUGH WHICH IT CAN STRAIN ITS FOOD.

WOODPECKERS AND FLICK-ERS HAVE STRONG BEAKS CAPABLE OF BORING INTO WOOD IN SEARCH OF IN-SECTS AND GRUBS.

SWALLOWS, SWIFTS, AND NIGHTHAWKS HAVE WIDE MOUTHS SUITED TO CATCH-ING INSECTS ON THE WING. TO ASSIST IN CAP-TURING THEIR PREY, THEY ALSO HAVE BRISTLES ON THE SIDES OF THEIR BEAKS.

FINCHES HAVE THICK SHORT BEAKS IDEALLY CONSTRUCTED FOR CRACK-ING SEEDS.

WILD TAILS

WESTERN CANADA'S WILDLIFE HAVE
BEEN ENDOWED WITH MANY KINDS
OF TAILS. SOME PERFORM SPECIFIC
TASKS AND ARE NOT SIMPLY THE FLY
SWISHERS THEY APPEAR TO BE. THE ALLIGATOR
LIZARD, FOR EXAMPLE, IS EQUIPPED WITH
A TAIL THAT SNAPS OFF WHEN THE
CREATURE IS CAUGHT BY A PREDATOR.
WHILE THE PREDATOR STOPS TO EAT THE TAIL, THE LIZARD SCURRIES AWAY
AND BEGINS GROWING A NEW ONE.

THE WHITETAIL DEER HOLDS ITS TAIL
ERECT AND WAVES IT FROM SIDE TO
SIDE WHEN DANGER THREATENS.
THE TAIL'S PURE WHITE UNDERSIDE
SERVES AS A WARNING FLAG TO
OTHER DEER.

THE BEAVER'S TAIL IS VERY
USEFUL INDEED. IT IS A PROP
WHILE CUTTING TREES, A
RUDDER WHILE SWIMMING,
AND AN ALARM SIGNAL WHEN
SLAPPED ON THE SURFACE
OF THE WATER.

WESTERN CANADA'S WOODPECKERS
HAVE STIFFLY SPINED TAIL FEATHERS
THAT ARE USED AS PROPS WHILE THE
BIRDS ARE BUSY DRILLING FOR WOOD-
BORING INSECTS. THE
TAIL IS ALSO
USED IN FLIGHT
AS A RUDDER.

THE OPPOSUM USES ITS
LONG HAIRLESS TAIL
AS AN AID IN CLIMB-
ING TREES. THIS
MAMMAL IS ALSO
THE ONLY ANIMAL
IN NORTH AMERICA
CAPABLE OF HANG-
ING BY ITS TAIL.

PLANKTON

THE MOST IMPORTANT FORM OF LIFE IN ANY POND, LAKE, OR SEA IS PLANKTON, THE BASIC FOOD SUPPLY OF THE UNDERWATER ENVIRONMENT. PLANKTON IS NOT A SPECIES OF LIFE BUT THOUSANDS AND THOUSANDS OF MICROSCOPIC PLANTS AND ANIMALS. A SMALL PAIL OF WATER MAY CONTAIN MILLIONS OF INDIVIDUALS AND IN- CLUDE THOUSANDS OF SPECIES. PLANKTON HAS LITTLE OR NO LOCOMOTIVE POWER BUT SIMPLY DRIFTS WITH THE CURRENT, PROVIDING FOOD FOR CREATURES RANG- ING IN SIZE FROM THE SHRIMP TO THE GREAT BLUE WHALE.

THE MOST NUMEROUS MEMBERS OF THE PLANKTON COMMUNITY ARE SINGLE-CELLED PLANTS CALLED DIATOMS. THESE MICRO- SCOPIC PLANTS REPRODUCE FAST- ER THAN ANY PLANTS ON LAND, AND WHERE DIATOMS FLOURISH ARE FOUND THE WORLD'S GREAT- EST FISHING GROUNDS.

THE ILLUSTRATIONS ON THIS PAGE SHOW SOME OF THE BIZARRE CHARACTERS IN THE PLANKTON WORLD. THEY ARE, OF COURSE, GREATLY MAGNI- FIED AND REPRESENT ONLY A FEW OF THE MANY THOUSANDS OF SPECIES.

A Selection of Other *Heritage House* Books

HISTORIC FRASER AND THOMPSON RIVER CANYONS: The Trans-Canada Highway from Vancouver to Kamloops is a unique route with scenery from mountains to sagebrush, wildlife from mountain goat to muskrat, vegetation from dogwood to cactus. Here is a 128-page guide — including its colorful history. **$7.95**

B.C. PROVINCIAL POLICE STORIES: For over 90 years from 1858 until 1950 the B.C. Provincial Police upheld the law. From official files here is a selection of the lawmen's most interesting adventures in mystery and murder. **$7.95**

WILDLIFE OF WESTERN CANADA: Over 100 illustrated panels on wildlife from the giant blue whale, at over 100 tons larger than the biggest dinosaur, to the pygmy shrew which weighs less than a soda cracker. **$8.95**

THE PICK OF THE NEIGHBOURHOOD PUBS — A GUIDED TOUR IN BRITISH COLUMBIA: There are over 230 of these home-like, folksy meeting places throughout B.C. In 160 pages with maps and photos here is a guide to some 100 of them. **$9.95**

OUTLAWS AND LAWMEN OF WESTERN CANADA — Volume One: Some of Western Canada's dramatic crimes. Includes Alberta Indian Swift Runner who ate his mother, brother, wife and six children; Saskatchewan's first stagecoach holdup; the 1880 death on duty of Manitoba's pioneer police chief; British Columbia's "Phantoms of the Rangeland," and many others. 128 pages, photos, maps. **$7.95**

OUTLAWS AND LAWMEN OF WESTERN CANADA — Volume Two: More of Western Canada's dramatic crimes. There is Jess Williams, in 1884 the first man hanged in Calgary; Saskatchewan's Almighty Voice whose murder of a policeman in 1895 caused six other deaths; B.C.'s Henry Wagner who in 1912 was hanged so quickly that he set a world record; and many others. 128 pages, photos, maps. **$7.95**

TRAGEDIES OF THE CROWSNEST PASS: In Canada no place equals the tragedies of the Crowsnest Pass on the Alberta-B.C. border. At Hillcrest a mine explosion killed 189 out of 235 men; at Frank a mountain collapsed, killing upward of 100 residents; and at Fernie a mine explosion killed 128 men. **$5.95**

OKANAGAN VALLEY: This guide reveals the many wonders of a valley of beaches and blossoms; wineries and history; sunshine and — perhaps — a genial Okanagan Lake resident called Ogopogo. 128 pages. **$7.95**

TALES OF CONFLICT: Indian-White Battles and Massacres in Pioneer B.C.: Contrary to popular belief, B.C. was not settled peacefully. Hundreds of whites and Indians died in murders and massacres from Vancouver Island to the Fraser Canyon, from the East Kootenay to the Chilcotin. 128 pages. **$7.95**

STAGECOACH AND STERNWHEEL DAYS IN THE CARIBOO AND CENTRAL B.C.: For 50 years from 1863 when the first stagecoach rumbled northward from Yale until 1921 when the sternwheeler *Quesnel* was destroyed in Fort George Canyon, colorful stagecoaches and sternwheelers served Central B.C. **$5.95**

SLUMACH'S GOLD — In Search of a Legend: Do the Coast Mountains some 40 miles northwest of Vancouver guard worth upwards of $100 million? **$3.95**

INCREDIBLE ROGERS PASS: In this 55-mile section of the Trans-Canada Highway over 200 men died keeping the CPR's main line open. Today snowsheds and artillery protect motorists from snowfall which can exceed 700 inches a year. **$3.95**

THE HOPE SLIDE — Disaster in the Dark: In the darkness 100 million tons of rock buried B.C.'s Southern Trans-Provincial Highway over 100 feet deep, engulfing motorists already trapped by a snow slide. **$3.95**

THE OVERLANDERS OF 1862: From Fort Garry the 150 gold seekers headed west in ox-carts for the goldfields of Cariboo, 1,500 wilderness miles away. Months later they arrived — speed 12 miles a day, five dead, the rest lucky to survive. **$3.95**

Bill Miner. . . STAGECOACH AND TRAIN ROBBER: The famous Pinkerton Detective Agency called him " . . . the master criminal of the American West." In a lifetime of crime he stole some $250,000, including $7,000 during Canada's first train holdup in B.C. in 1904 — and escaped from every jail he was in. **$4.95**

THE RIEL REBELLION — 1885: In 1870 Riel won the Metis representative government when the province of Manitoba was founded. In 1884-85 he again led the Metis. The results were tragic, with death to many — including Riel. **$5.95**

FROG LAKE MASSACRE: On April 17, 1885, came a message from what is today Alberta: "There's been a massacre at Frog Lake. All the white men have been murdered and their wives taken prisoners by Big Bear's Plains Crees." This book describes the massacres, pursuit of Big Bear, and the experiences of nearly fifty prisoners living under daily threat of execution. **$5.95**

CHUCKWAGON RACING — Calgary Stampede's Half Mile of Hell: Four wagons behind sixteen galloping horses chased by sixteen outriders makes chuckwagon racing one of the world's most dangerous sports. Born at the Calgary stampede in 1923, its heritage is the rangeland of the Canadian West. **$4.95**

The Death of ALBERT JOHNSON . . . Mad Trapper of Rat River: One intriguing mystery remains in this saga of pursuit and shoot-out in the numbing cold of Canada's Arctic over half a century ago — WHO WAS ALBERT JOHNSON? **$6.95**

Gabriel Dumont . . . Jerry Potts — CANADIAN PLAINSMEN: Had Dumont and Potts lived in the U.S., they would be as well known as Davy Crockett and Daniel Boone, frontiersmen whom Dumont and Potts equalled in skill and courage. **$3.95**

BANFF — PARK OF ALL SEASONS: A 15-square-mile reserve around a Rocky Mountain hotspring in 1885 developed into Banff National Park. Today Banff covers over 3,500 square miles and hosts over three million visitors a year. **$2.95**

MAJESTIC JASPER: Mt. Edith Cavell, Miette Hot Springs and Maligne Lake; wildlife from moose to mountain sheep; and year-round activities from skiing to hiking attract two million people yearly to this largest of Western National Parks. **$2.95**

WATERTON NATIONAL PARK: The Indians knew it as "Land of the Shining Mountains," a unique area in southwestern Alberta where prairie meets the mountains and nature sculpted lakes and valleys against a snow-peaked background. **$2.95**

MAGNIFICENT YELLOWHEAD HIGHWAY — Volume One: From Portage la Prairie to the Pacific Ocean, the Yellowhead is a panorama of prairie, plains and mountains. This volume describes 750 miles from Portage to Edmonton. **$2.95**

MAGNIFICENT YELLOWHEAD HIGHWAY — Volume Two: From Edmonton 504 miles through Jasper National Park to the sagebrush country of B.C. **$2.95**

MAGNIFICENT YELLOWHEAD HIGHWAY — Volume Three: From Mount Robson, the Rockies highest peak, westward 628 miles through some of North America's most scenic sport fishing country to tidewater at Prince Rupert. **$2.95**

STOPS OF INTEREST IN SOUTHERN ALBERTA: Along Alberta's highways are over 100 historical markers that describe unique geographical features, events of historical significance and honor pioneers. Here are those in southern Alberta. **$3.95**

THE CYPRESS HILLS OF ALBERTA-SASKATCHEWAN: Twenty miles wide, 200 miles long, nearly 5,000 feet high, they are a unique landform — ranking with the Grand Canyon and the desert of Western America. **$3.95**

GHOST TOWNS OF SOUTHERN ALBERTA — Volume One: Silver City, Bankhead, Mitford, Brant, Cleverville and other communities were once home to thousands. Today they survive only in photos, newspapers and memories. **$3.95**

GHOST TOWNS OF MANITOBA: During the surge of settlement scores of Manitoba towns were born. Scores also died. Some of them were Manitoba City, Bannerman, Odanah, Asessippi, Millwood, Ewart, Millford, Grand Valley, Dropmore and Hecla. Thirty-one chapters, over 100 photos, 160 pages. **$9.95**

The above titles and others are available at bookstores and other outlets throughout B.C., Alberta, Saskatchewan and Manitoba. If not available order direct from Heritage House Publishing Company, Box 1228, Station A, Surrey, B.C. V3S 2B3. Payment can be by cheque or money order. Books are shipped postpaid.